Havana Forever

UNIVERSITY PRESS OF FLORIDA

Florida A&M University, Tallahassee
Florida Atlantic University, Boca Raton
Florida Gulf Coast University, Ft. Myers
Florida International University, Miami
Florida State University, Tallahassee
New College of Florida, Sarasota
University of Central Florida, Orlando
University of Florida, Gainesville
University of North Florida, Jacksonville
University of South Florida, Tampa
University of West Florida, Pensacola

HAVANA

FOREVER

Havana Forever

A Pictorial and Cultural History of an Unforgettable City

Kenneth Treister, Felipe J. Préstamo, and Raul B. Garcia

Foreword by Ileana Ros-Lehtinen

Afterword by Jaime Suchlicki

University Press of Florida

Gainesville · Tallahassee · Tampa · Boca Raton

Pensacola · Orlando · Miami · Jacksonville · Ft. Myers · Sarasota

14 13 12 11 10 09   6 5 4 3 2 1

The publication of this book is made possible in part by a grant from
the Program for Cultural Cooperation between Spain's Ministry of Education
and Culture and United States Universities.

LIBRARY OF CONGRESS CATALOGING-IN-PUBLICATION DATA
Treister, Kenneth.
Havana forever: a pictorial and cultural history of an unforgettable city / Kenneth
Treister, Felipe J. Prestamo, and Raul B. Garcia; foreword by Ileana Ros-Lehtinen;
afterword by Jaime Suchlicki.
p. cm.
Includes bibliographical references and index.
ISBN 978-0-8130-3396-9 (alk. paper)
1. Havana (Cuba)—History. 2. Havana (Cuba)—Social life and customs.
3. Havana (Cuba)—Buildings, structures, etc. 4. Havana (Cuba)—Pictorial works.
I. Préstamo y Hernández, Felipe J. II. García, Raúl B. III. Title.
F1799.H34T74   2009
972.91'23—dc22
2009019228

Photo Credits
All photographs are by Kenneth Treister FAIA except: The University of Miami
Library, Cuban Heritage Collection—Fig. 18, Fig. 160, Fig. 161, Fig. 162, Fig. 163; the
University of Florida, Smathers Library, Special Collections—Fig. 29, Fig. 37, Fig 47,
Fig. 65, Fig. 81, Fig. 82, Fig. 83, Fig. 117, Fig. 151, Fig. 152, Fig. 153, Fig. 154, Fig. 155, Fig.
171, Fig. 172, Fig. 255; the Felipe J. Préstamo collection—Fig. 41, Fig. 42, Fig. 53, Fig. 57,
Fig. 64, Fig. 120, Fig. 101, Fig. 122; and historic post cards.

The University Press of Florida is the scholarly publishing agency for the State
University System of Florida, comprising Florida A&M University, Florida Atlantic
University, Florida Gulf Coast University, Florida International University, Florida
State University, New College of Florida, University of Central Florida, University of
Florida, University of North Florida, University of South Florida, and University of
West Florida.

University Press of Florida
15 Northwest 15th Street
Gainesville, FL 32611-2079
www.upf.com

To the memory of Felipe J. Préstamo, Cuban historian, who contributed his vast treasure-house of knowledge to this book and who loved Havana with all his heart. Felipe represented all that is good in the Cuban people, a people who, no matter where they live in the world, wear the Cuban flag on their sleeves and in their hearts.

Contents

Foreword

I was a child when we were uprooted from our home in Havana by a Communist revolution ushering in the Castro regime's murderous reign. We fled to safety and freedom in the United States, which welcomed us refugees with the warm embrace of compassion and understanding. As we flew over Havana and I looked out the small window of the Pan American Airlines plane, I saw shadows envelop the buildings of Cuba's capital city. The palm trees that adorned the Havana plazas were swaying in the wind as if bidding farewell to us, the waves crashing against "El Malecón," warning of what was to become of the "Mambo City" and the island nation known, until then, as "the Pearl of the Antilles." Our brief exile became permanent. Although a child, the aromas, images, and sounds of my birthplace were etched in my memory forever. My parents, nostalgic for Havana, would also love telling my brother and me about the people, places, and the way of life in pre-Communist Cuba. I treasure those stories, artifacts of what once was and what we hope will be again in Cuba one day.

For this reason, I was especially touched by this book, as the story of Havana's architecture so effectively mirrors the plight of the Cuban people under the Castro regime. Its beautiful descriptions of the rich and enchanting architectural history of old Havana allows readers to explore one of the most beautiful cities in the world. Using vibrant illustrations and insightful analysis, this book offers a unique opportunity to learn about Havana's rich history and culture. The varied legends of its landmark buildings and monuments provide us a glimpse of how much Havana has changed over the course of its history. Its old buildings, merely shells of their vibrant past, reflect the harsh realities of dictatorship on Cuba's society as a whole.

Two major themes run through *Havana Forever*: the "idealistic city," which describes the creative, imaginative, and surreal aspects of Havana and its architecture, and the theme of "flavoring of the city," which describes the energetic, rhythmical, and musical elements that have significantly influenced Cuban architecture, culture, and way of life.

At the outset, the book offers the reader a brief history of the origins of Havana and its Spanish roots. Havana's role in the Spanish colonial empire, which lasted more than 400 years, most heavily influenced the city's design and architecture. By the end of the sixteenth century, the evolution of trade routes in the West Indies had made Havana the main port for Central American explorers making the transatlantic voyage. Because of Spain's dominant role on the island, Havana was greatly influenced by a Mediterranean culture that emphasized vibrant music, architecture, and landscape. By the seventeenth century, the influence of Spanish designs on forts, churches, homes, and other public buildings was unmistakable. Most prominent are the churches: San Cristóbal, San Francisco de Asís, Iglesia Parroquial del Espíritu Santo, and San Agustin still stand as reminders of Cuba's rich Spanish heritage.

In the 1920s Havana's landscape was transformed by French landscape architect Jean Claude Nicolas Forestier. Prior to working in Havana, Forestier designed gardens in Paris, Spain, Morocco, and Lisbon, and completed a master plan for the redesign of public spaces in Buenos Aires. With his blueprint for Havana and his vision for broad avenues and parks, Forestier helped to remake Havana for a new century.

From Christopher Columbus and the bustling port that emerged from his voyage of discovery, to the architects and planners who envisioned such a beautiful city, modern Havana is a product of its glorious history. Sadly, the past fifty years of dictatorship under Fidel and Raul Castro and their Communist apparatchik have starved the island and left its timeless architecture a mere shell of its past. Havana's reemergence as free, democratic, and true to its enchanting past remains the hope for all of us who love Cuba and its great people. Until then, we have our wonderful memories, the stories of our parents, and this exceptional book.

Congresswoman Ileana Ros-Lehtinen*

* Ileana Ros-Lehtinen, U.S. House of Representatives; born in Havana, Cuba; Florida State House; Florida State Senate; elected as a Republican to the 101st Congress; reelected to the nine succeeding Congresses; first Hispanic woman and Cuban American to be elected to the U.S. Congress; ranking Republican, House Foreign Affairs Committee; Subcommittees on the Middle East and Central Asia, Africa, International Operations, Human Rights, and Western Hemisphere.

Reflections on a Magical City

The ballroom is heavy with the rich aroma of Cuban leaf and sweet, aged rum, and when the doors to the patio open, the faint perfume of the frangipani blossoms drifts in on a light Caribbean breeze. On this clear, starry night in Havana, through the soaring arches and clear crystal, a dancer in a spectacular splash of color mysteriously appears high in a tropical tree. Is she real or an illusion? Will I wake only to find it a dream? Let us dream together, for Havana is both a city of dreams and a city of memories.

This book is written by three architects who share a deep esteem for the city of Havana and a wish that it be preserved and respectfully enhanced in the years to come. Two are Cubans who studied, taught, and wrote about the beauty of Havana. The third author is an architect who has spent his life in South Florida and visited Havana. His visits span some fifty years and three distinct periods in its contemporary history, but he always repeated two things: he always stayed at the Hotel Nacional and visited the Cabaret Tropicana. On each visit he found a different veil spreading over the city, while the captivating essence of the city, nourished by its strong Cuban culture, remained unchanged.

The first visit was with high school friends in 1947 when Havana was, for visitors, the fun capital of the world. It flowed with spontaneity and life, both charming and harmonious. The Hotel Nacional was stately, with its broad windows opening wide onto the lights of the Malecón stretching out into the night like a string of pearls. The highlight was an evening at the Cabaret Tropicana and its Salon Arcos de Cristal, with its well-dressed patrons, spinning roulette wheels, and one memorable vision—a showgirl dancing high in a moonlit tree.

The second visit in 1957 was with his wife, when the city was rife with tension and soldiers were on guard everywhere. An innocent raising of a camera would bring an echoing response—the raising of a gun. Nevertheless, the city was beautiful and almost musical. The Hotel Nacional had kept its charm, and a return visit to the Tropicana was memorable, with gaming, fine dining, dancing, and, again, that beautiful showgirl spotlighted high in the tree. In many ways it seemed that nothing had changed.

Cabaret Tropicana, "Under the Stars" open-air terrace, where the bandstand is covered by this mathematical sculpture (1952) by architect Max Borges, who designed the award-winning Salon Arcos de Cristal at the Tropicana (1951).

The third visit was in 1997, when the city had been under Communist rule for some time. The city now was sad, with crumbling walls covered with the faded patina of neglect; however, behind the unpainted facade and propaganda signs, Havana was a city of extraordinary charm. The Hotel Nacional had been refurbished and had regained its special charm. A visit to the Tropicana was once more wonderful—even without the quiet shuffling of cards or the occasional joyful screams from the rolling dice—and the same tall, slender showgirl magically graced the same tropical tree.

Everything in Havana had changed, but, then again, nothing had changed.

Hotel Nacional loggia.

REFLECTIONS ON A MAGICAL CITY

Havana from the Castillo del Morro.

Preface

To properly read this book, you should be listening to the syncopated rhythm of the mambo, with blaring trumpets and the beat of the bongo, for Havana is not just a city, but a celebration of the Cuban way of life and its Creole roots. It is Cuba's persona, its history, culture, and unique people all combined into this historic city. Without the smug sophistication of many of the world's cities, the people of Havana—and the Cuban people in general—still possess a genuine warmth, friendliness, and zest for life that can be summed up and called the Cuban culture.

The integrated and total urbanistic aspects of Havana are of paramount importance to this book. The individual buildings, their architectural presence and urban spaces, by themselves do not necessarily create the wonderful living environment of Havana—it's the synergy of these elements. Havana is a city where space is often more important than mass.

Two prominent concepts are presented on these pages, and they are fairly independent of each other. One is the "ideal city," which is the artistic, inspired, magic, fantastic, or dreamlike aspects of Havana and its urban design. There is, perhaps, the hint of a similarity to the concept of "magic realism" found in the literature of Gabriel García Márquez. The other theme is the "city spice"—the vigorous, melodious, lyrical elements that include music, dancing, performance, even "cooking"—all architectural metaphors that emphasize the dynamics of architectural perception and cross-sensory parallels emanating from the strong influences of the very special phenomena that have evolved through time: the Cuban culture and the Cuban zest for life.

The story of Havana is not a story of architectural objects as a collection, as so many cities have become. Rather, Havana's synergy results from a symphony of stately buildings, each with its own patina of history gracing colonial streets that unveil their charms with each turn. Havana is an imaginative, interconnecting, and cross-referenced group of historic buildings within a unified, organic whole. It is a total "work of art," an example of *Gesamtkunstwerk* (the nineteenth-century concept of the totality of related art). What unfolds are enclosed urban plazas, colonnaded arcades, tree-shaded promenades, and gardens—all animated by Habaneros (the citizens of Havana). The English planner Gordon Cullen made the point when he wrote, "A city is more than the sum of its inhabitants. It has the power to generate a surplus of amenities, which is one reason why people like to live in communities rather that in isolation. . . . One building standing alone in the countryside is experienced as a work of architecture, but bring half a dozen buildings together and an art other than architecture is made possible."[1]

There is an old adage that it is better to be lucky than smart. Havana in some ways has become an important city by some strokes of good fortune. It is not the ultimate planned "smart" city like the palatial Versailles, Peter the Great's St. Petersburg, or Pierre L'Enfant's Washington, but rather a city that grew organically over many centuries of its dynamic history. The Havana of today resulted from three strokes of good fortune that eventually converged to make Havana a city of wealth.

First was the sheer luck of geography. Due to its location as one of the gateways to the Caribbean, Cuba was chosen by the Spanish Crown to be one of its links in the chain that connected its vast American empire to the motherland. Cuba was the largest of the Caribbean islands, less than ninety miles from the Florida Keys, and strategically located to control the entrance to the Gulf of Mexico.

Havana's second stroke of fortune was that the Spanish conquered all of South and Central America and Mexico, except for Brazil. Spain then funneled most of the wealth of gold and silver stolen from the treasure trove of Mexico and Peru through the port of Havana, the collection port where large convoys of sailing ships assembled before they started their perilous journey across the vast Atlantic to Spain. A little of this wealth peeled off and stayed in Havana.

The third item of good fortune was that with ample fresh water and rich soil, Cuba could produce an abundance of fine agricultural products. With land from the king and labor from slavery, Cuba's plantation economy prospered. The port of Havana prospered from exporting sugar, rum, tobacco, coffee, copper, and honey (rum was initially made by Spanish colonists from the juice of sugarcane plants in Puerto Rico in the 1500s). Three of these crops—tobacco, sugar, and rum—were, to varying degrees, addictive. Europe and most of the civilized world craved these luxury products. With this income from agriculture, plus that derived from shipbuilding and repairs, wealth flowed into the mansions of Havana.

Daniel Burnham, the architectural creator of the White City, Chicago's World's Columbian Exposition of 1893, said, "Make no little plans, for they have no power to stir man's minds."[2] When it came to the creation of Havana, there were three grand dreams, fuzzy inspirational yearnings, and images that took on a life of their own and evolved with every new generation. The dreamers did not intentionally start out to create a world-class city, but their collected actions over time created Havana. First was Christopher Columbus, who, with stunning audacity, set out across an unexplored ocean in three tiny ships seeking fortune and plunder. He challenged people's limits and changed the world, but, in so doing, destroyed so much. Then there was the Spanish royalty, who made Havana one of their main links in their

The chapel of the Fortaleza de San Carlos de la Cabaña.

Havana, a city where reflection pools, coral rock, and tropical vines soften the urban landscape. Here the Castillo de la Real Fuerza presents beautiful Spanish military architecture with sharp angles and textures, all with the mellow patina of age reflected in its moat.

vast American empire. Last there were the fighters for Cuban independence who were part of the struggle that created a new republic. Havana then became Cuba's capital, a city that was to epitomize a new beginning and a new nation.

Havana today is frozen in time and space, but it is a city still saturated with the hidden beat of Afro-Cuban music, a petrified city under siege, spared by the unintended blessings of an economic stagnation born out of the forced isolation due to the Communist revolution. It has therefore been saved from the destruction that often comes with the twentieth century's modern architecture, where buildings are created as entities unto themselves that owe nothing to the neighborhood or city to which they belong. This is the tragedy of contemporary architecture today. Havana has also been saved from the destabilizing effects of uncontrolled suburban sprawl and the all-conquering automobile with its all-consuming concrete ribbons that have ravaged the cities of the world.

Havana, even now as it wears the mantle of neglect, is a city that has the potential of being both fun-loving and spontaneous—a city that mixes its Spanish and African ancestry well; a city of intrigue, nostalgia, and romance, where centuries of dynamic history meld together to form a hauntingly, magical city; a city that once seemed endowed with eternal youth but has now taken on the pallor of old age; a city of faded walls and depressed spirits. Today life hides among the ruins, where the select few once lived in splendor and where now a multitude of small, human vignettes are played out each day in the crumbling mansions of Habana Vieja (Havana's Old City)—a play without an audience because all the residents are unwilling actors forced to follow a script not of their choosing. Havana is a city waiting to be reborn and hopefully not destroyed.

There are basically two broad elements that make a great city. First, a city is the "deterministic product" of its historical events and the factors of it economic, technological, social, and cultural conditions. Second, a city is the "realization of dreams," a matter of vision, aspiration, dedication, effort, struggle, and sacrifice. It is a product guided by human consciousness that tells us about where we came from and what we can become.

Havana is a wonderful city, even a poetic, impressionistic city. There are only a few cities in the world that can be described today as human from the cultural, architectural, and urbanistic points of view. The number of these cities, ones that are both intrinsically cultural and beautiful, is becoming smaller with each passing day, and this mantle may some day pass from Havana as well. Frank Lloyd Wright, the luminary American architect, once said, "A civilization is only a way of life. A culture is the way of making the way of life beautiful."

Havana developed over many centuries into a fine and noble city by the correlation and orchestration of many elements of what can be collectively called the

Cuban culture. Havana is an organic city of natural growth often affected by military and political upheavals and no small amount of greed, land speculation, and the creation of new *repartos* (planned neighborhoods).

This wonderful city was not created by the "fancy of one man" or formulated by one great plan or even a series of great plans but as a reaction to a sequence of improvised circumstances, an unremitting, natural, organic process. It developed not by pure chance where people let things just happen, but rather by a continuous response over the years by people who cared, who dared to dream and dared to hope. These people, by their collective will, seemed to have that ill-defined notion of how to move the city in the right direction. It was this step-by-step creation, a communal response to time and circumstance, that allowed the accumulated forces to move Havana almost mysteriously in the right direction.

The purpose here is to understand the qualities of Havana's architecture and urban culture. Havana now finds itself at a crucial time in its history, perhaps its ultimate crossroads. It faces the threat of being lost, not only for Cubans but for all humanity as well. The urgency to save and properly restore Havana as a living city has never been greater. This book presents the history and exemplary urban qualities of Havana's urban concept that should not be lost, for they hold the key to its future preservation as an archetypal city.

Havana's portrait is presented in five parts, through different but interrelated lenses. In Part I, we look at its architectural and urban history, for its history envelopes every facet of its being. Part II describes its rich Spanish traditions in architecture and public spaces, where the city's spaces are often more important than its buildings. Part III examines the city's distinct neighborhoods, the essential marrow of all great cities. Part IV views the influences on the city's development and its architectural landmarks. Part V explores the city's urban characteristics, its colorful spirit, music, and nightlife and expresses the magic of a pedestrian city to demonstrate the importance of Cuban culture via an urban and architectural perspective.

Harmony reigned in Havana's parks and squares. Beyond this simple fountain in the garden of the Plaza de Armas sits the Palacio del Segundo Cabo (1770). Originally designed and used as the city post office, it was the seat of the Senate in the early republic and now houses the Instituto Cubano del Libro (Cuban Book Institute).

Following page: Monument to Francisco de Frias y Jacott, who since 1848 was called Conde de Pozos Dulces (1809-1877). He inherited the title given to his grandfather in 1790 by King Carlos IV. In 1859 he and his family transformed their family farm, El Carmelo, into a large section of what became El Vedado. He participated in the allocation of land for the Colon Cemetery and helped both modernize farming and the study of the Cuban economy. This monument, located at Calle Linea and Avenue L, Vedado, was built in 1916 by Cuban president Mario García Menocal.

Part I

Havana's Urban and Architectural History

The city of Havana today.

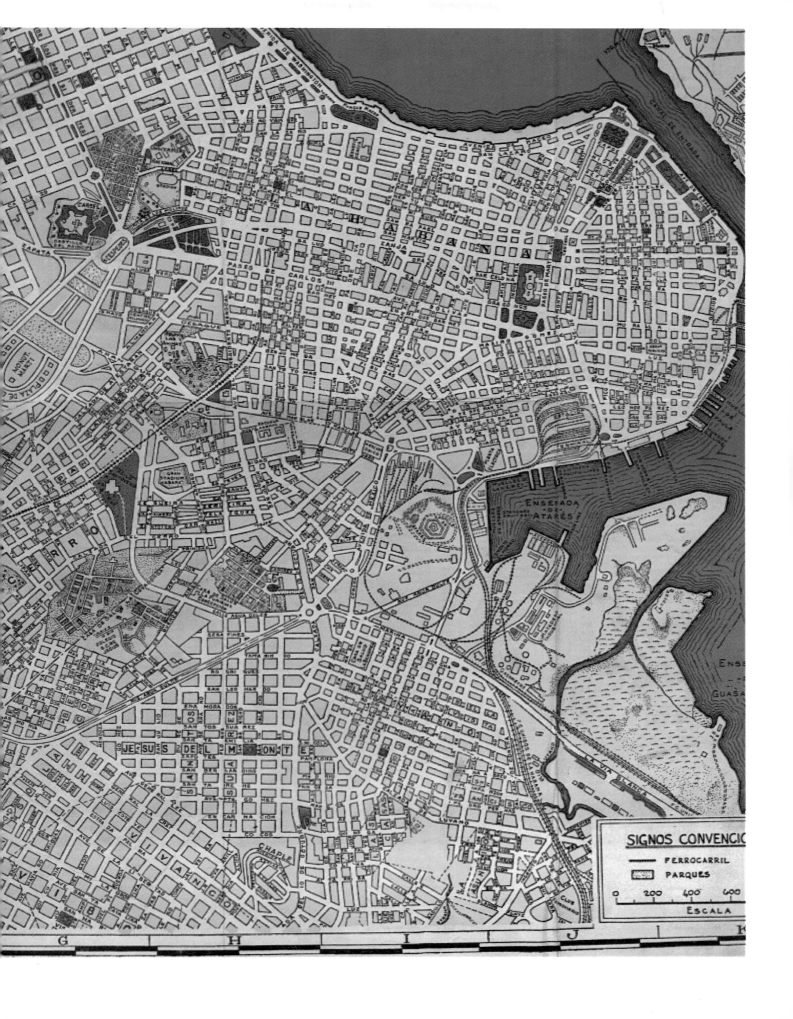

The Fortaleza de San Carlos de la Cabaña.

Prologue to the History of Havana

To understand the urban presence and architecture of Havana, one has to appreciate its urban growth, history, and culture, for no city evolves in isolation. Instead, a city reflects its past, its ecology, and its citizens and their dreams. History can be presented through different lenses—one can view history through the lenses of economic development, conflicts and wars, or politics, for example—but here we see and explore Havana through the filters of urban and architectural development.

To begin the story of Havana, one should understand the conditions prevailing in Spain at the time of its discovery of the New World. Spain was a country where violence and church-sponsored cruelty, manifested in the torturer's rack of the Inquisition, pervaded daily life. Spain had expelled its Jews, and the powerful Catholic crowns of Castile and Aragón had unified Spain and driven the Moors from its shores. As the fifteenth century ebbed, advances in navigation and shipbuilding made long-distance sea travel and commerce feasible. The seafaring countries of Portugal and Spain led this new age of exploration and trade.

By virtue of experience and achievement, the Portuguese were entitled to lead in the exploration of the New World; however, a single man's vision hurdled that advantage by convincing the Spanish sovereigns that untold riches lay beyond the Atlantic. Spain's faith in Christopher Columbus and its willingness to sponsor his dream trumped Portugal's prior experience and achievements in the realm of exploration. In 1492 vast stretches of the Atlantic Ocean were unknown, a void waiting to be explored. Now it was time to fill that void with one pure act of exploration that started with one man's dream.[1]

The Mediterranean and Caribbean

The mechanics of sea travel from Europe to the unknown lands across the Atlantic Ocean in the fifteenth century were governed by two simple principles: trade winds and currents. Until the nineteenth century, sailing ships traveled at the whim of currents and wind—one had little other choice. In the Atlantic Ocean, both the trade winds and currents make a giant, clockwise circle, called the North Atlantic Current, around its center. From the Caribbean, it cuts northeast across the Atlantic, an extension of the Gulf Stream, and then doubles back toward the Equator on its underside in what is called the Atlantic conveyor belt, with a volume of water thirty times greater than all the rivers of the world. Sailing ships leaving Europe and traveling west had to ride these currents and prevailing winds in this broad circle, first to the Canary Islands and then west, finding landfall in the Caribbean islands. The currents then follow the Gulf Stream up the Florida coast and then turn back to the North Atlantic and Europe, completing a giant circle. It was not the continental coast of the United States that was initially important, as we are often taught in American schools with the story of the *Mayflower* and Pilgrims, but rather the sandy shores of the Caribbean. For example, in Barbados, the most eastern and therefore the first island to welcome the ships from Europe, the population in 1655 was 43,000 people, while New York City had only 1,000 inhabitants. By 1770 New York had grown to 25,000, while Barbados had 109,200 souls.

Of the many Caribbean islands that greeted Europe's great sailing ships, Cuba was the largest—the tropical paradise that Columbus discovered on his first voyage in 1492. Havana, when it eventually became Cuba's capital, evolved into an important link in the chain of Spain's exploitation of New World wealth, which was mainly exploited from Mexico and Peru. Havana enjoyed special advantages as one of Spain's important hubs for the transfer of people, gold, and silver back to the homeland.

In return, Havana became infused with Mediterranean culture, which in the fifteenth century was based on the sea and trade. Part of this Mediterranean culture carried over to the Spanish Caribbean in the form of the rich life of Spain, particularly of Andalusia. Here the Islamic love of music, architecture, and landscape created a unity in form and style.[2]

In the Andalusian cities of the Moors, homes were hidden behind walls or adjacent buildings, a continuity of form found coincidently in harmonious music. This "hidden architecture" is found today in Habana Vieja, where, aided by the patina of time, there is a continuity of hidden charm that has not been destroyed by the modernists, whose buildings often shout for attention at the expense of continuity and harmony within the neighborhood. The happy sound of water from a central fountain in a patio in Habana Vieja is pure Andalusia.

Now let us look at the living legacy of the past, at the unique identity and nature of Havana and what is embodied in its formative structure and its most precious historic artifacts.

Chapter 1

From Village to Walled City (1519–1762)

Habana Vieja. Early Havana was a city of simple Spanish colonial architecture. Here
we see the shaded open balcony of the Casa de Martín Aróstegui (1759).

SAN CRISTÓBAL DE LA HABANA was settled in July 1515 by Diego Velázquez de Cuéllar, a Spanish conquistador and the first governor of Cuba. It is thought to have been located on the Broa Inlet near current-day Batabanó on the southern coast of Cuba. That site was abandoned after a few years, and in 1519 the settlers relocated to a site near the mouth of the Almendares River on the northern coast of Cuba. This location, too, was considered unsuitable, and the small settlement was relocated again later that same year, this time to the present location on the shores of Puerto de Carenas (Careening Bay), now called Bahía de Havana (Havana Bay).

At this time, Cuba was considered little more than a convenient staging area for expeditions into more promising areas of the New World. With few natural resources, and with the gold found in the riverbanks not representing any great wealth, Cuba's value to the Spanish conquistadores rested in its convenient location at the mouth of the Gulf of Mexico, the gateway to the legendary wealth of the New World. San Cristóbal de Habana was a small village with a population of around fifty Spanish families and a small number of Indians. The Indians were resettled a few years later to a site across the bay, which is today the city of Guanabacoa. The first houses were primitive huts built in the style of the Indian dwellings: constructed of sun-dried mud sheltered by palm-leaf thatch roofs.

Residents engaged in fishing and rudimentary agriculture and lived in huts aligned along a few dirt roads. This poor settlement was attacked and destroyed in 1555 by the French pirate Jacques de Sores. Cuban historian José María Bens Arrarte assessed the losses to be of little value, but the destruction of the settlement gave residents and authorities the opportunity to rectify initial mistakes in the design and development of the village.

By this time, Spain had acquired a better understanding of the characteristics of its New World holdings and began developing basic procedures for the management of these colonies. The city of Santo Domingo (Dominican Republic) was the center of the colonial empire in this initial phase of colonization of the New World—before the conquest of Mexico—and it influenced the development of Havana in terms of management and urban design. Spain designated Don Alonso de Cáceres, a judge in the audiencia of Santo Domingo, as *oidor* (one who listens) to the Cuban colony. Cáceres crafted ordinances late in 1519 for public administration and regulations for street design and land subdivision. These regulations became precedents for other colonies in the Americas in the development of new cities.

Cáceres's ordinances guided the slow rebuilding of Havana after Jacques de Sores had destroyed the city. Streets were realigned, and land divisions were better organized. One of the most positive results was the designation of a parcel of land in front of the small church of the village as a plaza. Cáceres's ordinances preceded the famous Spanish Laws of the Indies, which dictated how towns in the New World colonies were to be developed, by many years.

A Better Route to Spain

A most important event occurred late in 1519: pilot Antón de Alaminos discovered a new route for returning to Spain. Alaminos, a member of Hernán Cortés's troops who came to America in one of the Colón (Columbus) trips, had vast experience in ocean travel.

Cortés decided to inform the king of his discovery of the wealth of Mexico as a way to consolidate his power and ordered Alaminos to deliver the news to Spain, bypassing Velázquez in Cuba. To accomplish this, Alaminos decided to navigate north following the Gulf Stream and then turn east along the Atlantic currents and trade winds. Alaminos's trip established the future navigation route from Mexico and Tierra Firme toward Spain. Havana, strategically placed, therefore became an important location in this new Calle Real de las Indias (Royal street of the Indies).

At the end of the sixteenth century, Spain realized that the port of Havana was a basic component in the empire, but it lacked the proper military protection. The defense of the port and the city of Havana led to unprecedented military plans, which created a Spanish military stronghold in the Americas that lasted for more than two centuries. The recognition of the importance of Havana attracted the interest of many religious orders, which, during the same period, built hospitals, convents, churches, and schools, complementing the urbanization of the city.

José María Bens Arrarte divided this historical period of Havana into three phases: first, the city of the carpenter, from settlement to the destruction by Jacques de Sores; second, the military city, dominated by the construction of the defenses of the city; and, third, the religious city, when most of the initial churches were completed.

The Military City

The first fortress built in Havana was La Fuerza Vieja (the Old Force). Completed on May 12, 1540, it was poorly designed, was incorrectly located, and had serious deficiencies in its construction methods and materials. The fortress was destroyed by the French pirate de Sores in his 1555 attack and rebuilt in another location.

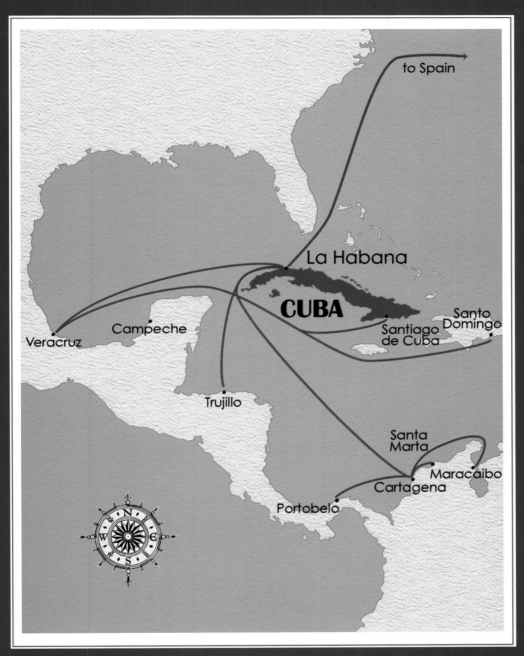

By the end of the sixteenth century, the evolution of the trade routes in the West Indies and the introduction of the navigation route from Mexico to Spain through the Florida Straits had made Havana the main port for convoys attempting the perilous Atlantic Ocean crossing.

The Castillo de la Real Fuerza and its reflection in its tranquil moat.

The new fortress was called Castillo de la Real Fuerza (Castle of the Royal Force), designed by military engineer Bartolomé Sánchez. Sánchez arrived in Havana in 1558 and was appointed by King Felipe II to rebuild the city's defenses. Construction was initiated in 1558 and completed in 1577 with the help of slaves, prisoners, and money from the colony of Mexico. The fortress's circular tower (1632) is adorned by a bronze weathervane, La Giraldilla, sculpted by Gerónimo Martín Pinzón, of a maiden thought to be Doña Isabel de Bobadilla, the wife of Hernando de Soto, which has become a symbol of the city. La Real Fuerza still stands today as a landmark in colonial Habana Vieja's Plaza de Armas.

The First Spanish Town Square

Bartolomé Sánchez came to Havana accompanied by a large group of experienced construction workers who elevated the quality of work in the city. However, an unexpected impact on Havana was the reaction of the residents when they saw the land previously designated for a public plaza now being utilized by the new fortress.

Residents of Havana, at that time a poor, isolated village, decided to send a letter to the king of Spain asking for a new plaza for the city. At the official meeting of the municipal government held at the *cabildo* (town hall), it was recorded that the residents presented a letter to the king requesting "a plaza for the city, because the site reserved for that use was taken by the Castillo de la Fuerza so there is no plaza in this town, so important for Spain, a destination of fleets and ships of your majesty. This town does not have now a place to celebrate 'corridas de toros,' a place where we can celebrate the success and victories that God our Lord gives to your Majesty."[1]

This petition for a new plaza from the residents of a poor town isolated from the rest of the world is a unique example of the strength of the urban image that the residents of Havana carried from Spain. Years later the residents of Havana got their new plaza, a site next to La Fuerza, the present-day Plaza de Armas.

The Fortresses Castillo del Morro, Castillo de la Punta, and the City Walls

The completion of the Castillo de la Real Fuerza did not satisfy the military's defensive needs for Havana, and the city's residents convinced the king to order the construction of two more fortresses: one on a hill in front of the city at the entrance of the bay, the Castillo de los Tres Reyes del Morro (Morro Castle, 1589–1630), and one on the opposite site of the entrance to the bay, Castillo de San Salvador de la Punta.

Castillo de la Real Fuerza in the Plaza de Armas. The first bastioned fortress built in America, it replaced an earlier fort destroyed in 1555 and rebuilt between 1558 and 1577 by slaves and French prisoners. The sharp, angular ramparts of the Castillo eventually were joined to the Plaza de Armas.

Bautista Antonelli, an Italian military engineer who had successfully worked for the Spanish kings Carlos V and Felipe II, designed the two castles. Castillo del Morro (1589–1630) was the largest and most successfully designed of all the Spanish fortresses in America up to this time. It had become part of the image of Havana known around the world. Castillo de San Salvador de la Punta (1589–circa 1600) did not receive the same military fame but was considered a necessary complement to Castillo del Morro. A large lighthouse, Faro del Morro, was built in 1844 and has guided ship captains into Havana Bay ever since.

Castillo del Morro was a powerful figure dominating the image of the city with potent defenses: two batteries, Los Doce Apóstoles and the Pastora, plus all the traditional facilities of a fortress of that era. However, the Spanish military considered that the three castles were still not enough to protect Havana and insisted on building defensive walls (Las Murallas) around the city. After the walls were built, the city became a self-contained walled city of human scale and relative isolation. Construction of the walls was officially initiated on February 1674 and finalized in 1740, 182 years after they were proposed for the first time.[2] Similar to Barcelona's example designed by Ildefons Cerdà after the demolition of that city's walls, Havana's walls had a total length of three miles, with an average width of five feet.

Cristóbal de Roda, the military engineer who succeeded Antonelli, designed the walls to encircle Havana, proposing at the same time an urban plan for the city inside. The walls were roughly parallel to de Roda's plan; however, they were located several blocks inland, and their height was increased to ten feet. The area inside the walls could accommodate more than 3,500 soldiers and 180 pieces of artillery. When completed, the walls had nine gates; however, more were added through the years to facilitate the movement of the growing population.

The first gate to the city's walls was the Puerta la Muralla, located next to the street of the same name; it was also called the Puerta de Tierra. Another initial gate was La Punta, near the Castillo de la Punta. One of the most utilized entries to the city was the Puerta de Monserrate located near Obispo and O'Reilly streets, an entrance rich in architectural embellishments. The walls were demolished starting on August 8, 1863, after 123 years of use, when it was determined that they served no military purpose.

The Religious City

After fortifying the city, Havana turned its attention as an expression of Spain's pious devotion to establishing a large number of religious institutions, most of which are still standing today in Habana Vieja. The first church, called San Cristóbal, was

Castillo de los Tres Reyes del Morro and its lighthouse (Faro del Morro, 1844) guarding the entrance to the Bay of Havana, perhaps the best-known landmark of the city.

The Castillo de los Tres Reyes del Morro and its lighthouse (Faro del Morro, 1844) seem to grow out of and be an integral part of the stone cliff at the entrance to the Canal de Entrada to the Bahía de la Habana (entrance canal to Havana Bay).

built on the current site of the Palacio de los Capitanes Generales (Palace of the Governors), but subsequently was destroyed by pirates in 1638.

Of the many notable convents and churches built in Habana Vieja, San Francisco de Asís (1574–1591, rebuilt in 1730) was one of the first and most important (discussed in chapter 2). Iglesia Parroquial del Espíritu Santo (Parish Church of the Holy Ghost) is the city's oldest standing church, founded in 1632 and located on the corner of Calles Cuba and Acosta. It was originally dedicated to the Holy Spirit as a hermitage for the devotions of free blacks.[3] Today it is one of Havana's most beautiful churches. This church has been remodeled periodically over the centuries, with Bishop Gerónimo Valdés, abbot of the order of San Basilio, providing the most dramatic improvements during his twenty-three years of building religious institutions in Havana.

After their initial religious use, many of the churches and convents were converted to commercial or governmental use. Iglesia San Agustin (Church of St. Augustine) was built in 1608 and later was converted into the Banco del Comercio. Convento de Santa Clara de Asís (Convent of St. Clair of Assisi), one of Havana's oldest, was founded in 1644 for cloistered nuns who, once they entered, lived and died within the convent, having no relationship with the outside world. It was later enlarged to include the Sailor's House, built by a wealthy naval officer for his daughter after a failed love affair. The city's first slaughterhouse, public fountain, public baths, and the Public Works Department were located here.

Casa Cuna, an orphanage, was built in 1687 by Bishop Diego de Compostela, whose name still marks one of the city's streets, a street that at one time was crowded with five religious institutions. Bishop Gerónimo Valdés later relocated the orphanage to another building. All the children from this orphanage took the name Valdés to honor him.

Havana's cathedral, Catedral de la Virgen María de la Inmaculada Concepción (Cathedral of the Virgin Mary of the Immaculate Conception), belonging to the Jesuits, was completed in 1777 after the Jesuits were banished from Spain and its dominions in 1767 (discussed in chapter 2).

Some of Havana's notable religious institutions are Iglesia y Convento de Nuestra Señora de Belén (Church and Convent of Our Lady of Bethlehem), built by Federico Miahle; Iglesia y Convento de Santa Clara de Asís, Havana's first nunnery; Iglesia del Santo Ángel Custodio (Church of the Guardian Angel), built by Diego de Compostela in 1687 on Angel Hill and later rebuilt in a neo-Gothic style in the nineteenth century, where José Martí was baptized in 1853; Iglesia y Convento de Nues-

Catedral de la Virgen María de la Inmaculada Concepción in the Plaza de la Catedral. Its rhythmic, scrolled, and undulating facade makes it the perfect example of the Cuban baroque style.

tra Señora de la Merced (Church and Convent of Our Lady of Mercy), construction of which started in 1637 and continued into the next century; Iglesia de Santo Cristo Buen Viaje (Church of the Good Voyage), built in 1732 as a place where sailors could pray for a safe journey; Seminario de San Carlos y San Ambrosio (Seminary of Saint Charles and Saint Ambrose), the eighteenth-century companion and neighbor to the Catedral; and Iglesia del Sagrado Corazón de Jesús (Church of the Sacred Heart of Jesus), whose 253-foot neo-Gothic bell tower was consecrated in 1923.

Casa de los Marquéses de Aguas Claras (built in the second half of the sixteenth century). The second floor forms an arched opening for the Restaurante La Fuente del Patio, which opens to the Plaza de la Catedral.

Catedral de la Virgen María de la Inmaculada Concepción. The heavy and dominating twin towers may seem to be symmetrical but are not, with different heights, widths, and details.

Chapter 2

Growth and Change in the Walled City (1763–1863)

England's Victory in Havana Generated a New Defense Plan (1763–1779)

Plaza de Armas and the Palacio de los Capitanes Generales—a blend of harmonious architecture and a pedestrian-friendly public square.

The British Invasion

In the latter part of the sixteenth century, England looked with envy at the enormous wealth flowing to Spain's coffers from Spain's New World Caribbean possessions. At first England sent Sir Francis Drake, a brilliant corsair, who captured Santo Domingo and Cartagena and who passed Havana on his way to destroy the Spanish fortifications being built at St. Augustine. In the seventeenth century, the Dutch and English worked together to establish colonies in the Caribbean. The rush for colonies by the English, French, and Dutch created a new and growing challenge for Spain. England took Jamaica in 1655, thereby increasing Cuba's vulnerability to the English.

England declared war on Spain on January 4, 1762, and one of its first strategies was to gain control of Havana, one of Spain's richest and most important prizes in the Americas.[1] At first overshadowed by the immense wealth of precious metals found in other parts of the New World, Cuba had come into its own as a precious commodity initially through its prime location as a gathering point for ships laden with riches from Peru and Mexico and later from the Philippines and the Far East. Ships traveling alone to Spain were easy targets for pirates, so royal decree mandated travel by convoy. In this way, Havana's harbor became a busy center of commerce, handling immense wealth from the New World. Cubans initially profited by supplying the ships with basic necessities, food and tobacco, but as the traffic through the port increased, the sophistication of the trade did so as well, until Havana became desirable not only as a strategic rallying point for Spanish ships but also for trade on its own merits.

The British thought El Morro and its defenses were vulnerable, so in June 1762 a large convoy of British warships, perhaps the largest ever assembled in the Caribbean, with 11,000 troops aboard, attacked Havana. In addition to an epidemic of yellow fever in its garrison, Havana indeed proved to be poorly defended, and the British took the city. The British flag flew over Havana for six months. Then, on February 10, 1763, France, Spain, and England signed the Treaty of Paris, in which British-controlled Cuba was exchanged for Spain's Florida peninsula.

The Three Castles

The short period of time Havana was under British domination (1762–1763) had a major impact on the relationship between Madrid and Cuba. Spain, deciding that military defenses were not enough to maintain Spanish control of this important part of the empire, adopted a new military strategy based on the construction of a defensive triangle outside the city. This consisted of a fortress in each angle: Fortaleza San Carlos de la Cabaña, Castillo del Príncipe, and Santo Domingo de Atarés. The new castles were constructed between 1763 and 1779, completing the most advanced military defenses of any city in the Americas at that time. As these military plans were implemented, Havana started to become a real city. It was organized into barrios (neighborhoods), its houses were numbered, many of its streets were paved, and the city's urban services were improved.

The first of the castles to be built was Fortaleza San Carlos de la Cabaña (1774), named in honor of Carlos III, king of Spain. Designed by military engineer Silvestre Abarca, the Fortaleza de San Carlos de la Cabaña was built at the point where British forces took the city in 1762, a site that military experts always considered to be a critical location for the defenses of Havana (see a more complete discussion in chapter 1). A cannon is still fired from the Fortaleza de San Carlos de a Cabaña every night at nine, the original signal for the closing of Havana's gates and the raising of the chain that sealed its harbor.

The second castle to be constructed was Castillo del Príncipe (1779), located on top of Aróstegui Hill, which dominated a large area at the outskirts of the city. The design of the fortress is an irregular pentagon, which was adapted to the topography of the site. It had the capacity to house 900 soldiers, one of the largest contingents to be used in defending the city at any one location. It was built from 1767 to 1779.

The third castle that would finalize the defenses was Santo Domingo de Atarés (1767), built on top of Soto Hill near the end of the bay. Santo Domingo de Atarés was designed by the military engineers Agustin Cramer and Silvestre de Abarca. This is the lesser known of the three castles, but a proper and necessary component of the defenses of Havana.

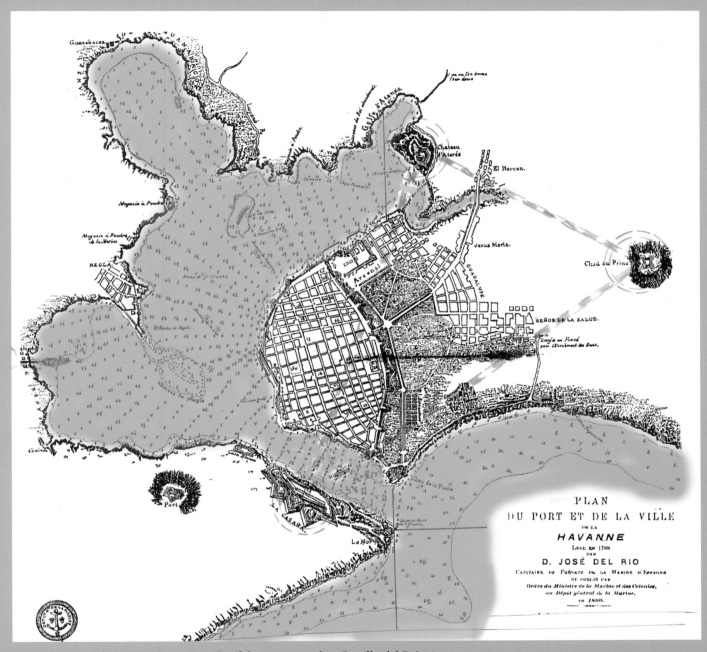

Havana's new defense strategy, a triangle of three new castles: Castillo del Príncipe, Fortaleza San Carlos de la Cabaña, and Santo Domingo de Atarés.

Fortaleza San Carlos de la Cabaña. The strong geometric patterns are created when simple utilitarian details, such as the steps and adjoining stonework, are combined with strong sunlight.

Fortaleza San Carlos de la Cabaña—the brutal and monumental architecture of geometric forms.

The Urban Life of the City under the Marqués de la Torre

After the completion of the military fortifications, Spain was concerned with the improvement of the urban quality of life and its architecture in Havana. Felipe de Fondesviela y Ondeano, Marqués de la Torre, governor of Cuba from 1771 to 1777, was the leader of this initiative. He was part of the Spanish Enlightenment and is considered the first, and probably the best, urbanist of colonial Havana.

Governor General de la Torre was so concerned with the conditions of Havana that he considered it a city in name only. De la Torre commented in a letter to a Spanish friend that the city was like a *caserío* (small village). Its houses were constructed with thatch roofs and adobe walls, the plazas were covered by weeds, and, most of the time, it was flooded. The city did not have a *paseo* (promenade) or a theater. The only entertainment were the religious processions, military parades, or a walk at night along Muralla and Mercaderes streets, full of small bazaars and illuminated by small *quinqués* (lights) creating the merry looks of a fair.[2]

De la Torre decided that a *paseo* could enhance the urban life of residents and visitors, so he hired engineer Antonio Fernández de Trebejos to design "a balcony" for the city in front of the port.[3] Trebejo's design was to have a simple walkway between the hospital, the Church of San Francisco, and a site that was later used for the first theater of Havana, El Teatro Principal.

El Teatro Principal

The cultural center of the city for many years, El Teatro Principal was compared favorably with similar buildings in Madrid, offering for the first time in the city the opportunity of enjoying professional theatrical presentations. Paseo del Prado and Alameda de Paula were improved many times during the urban development of Havana, and today are an important part of the city's heritage.

The Beginning of Paseo del Prado Boulevard

As Havana continued to grow, the residents were attracted to the area outside the walls as a place to enjoy the open land between the walls and the emerging housing in what was later called the Ensanche (expansion), the area of the city's enlargement, or the *barrio de extramuros* (the neighborhood outside the walls).[4] De la Torre ordered the clearing of a corridor parallel to Las Murallas, from La Punta Door in the north to the Puerta de Tierra in the south. He also ordered the planting of trees along this path to provide shade for those who would enjoy a stroll or a

Habana Vieja—the ecclesiastical and civil center of Spanish colonial Havana.

carriage outing. This poplar-lined promenade outside the city walls was originally called the Alameda de Isabella II in honor of the Spanish queen. Later the name was changed to Paseo de Martí, in honor of Cuba's national hero, and finally to Paseo del Prado. It is commonly called *paseo*, or the Prado, using as its precedent the famous late-eighteenth-century boulevard Paseo del Prado in Madrid. The Paseo del Prado in Havana was remodeled and improved in the nineteenth century and in 1929 by Jean Claude Nicolas Forestier (1861–1930) to be similar to the wonderful promenade in Barcelona's las Ramblas (see chapters 7, 10, and 13).

Habana Vieja

Habana Vieja was built as both the ecclesiastical and civil center of this proud Spanish colonial capital. After the nine o'clock curfew, the city gates were closed, confining the Habaneros (citizens of Havana) within the city's massive defensive walls. A city enclosed by such walls is introverted by nature and has, in addition to the advantage of security, the benefit of being well defined, compact, and well integrated. Habana Vieja was a city graced by beautiful urban plazas and aristocratic mansions that for 350 years comprised the entire city of Havana. This urban center was made up of a compact grid of narrow and irregular cobblestone streets with a plan predating the Spanish Crown's main planning ordinances for its colonial empire, the Law of the Indies.

The original walled city has the natural, organic characteristic of a Spanish medieval town rather than the more rigid, formal plan of most Spanish colonial cities. The narrow streets are an ancestral remnant of the village streets of the Moors of North Africa and their cousins in the Andalusian towns of Spain. These towns and villages followed the Mediterranean tradition of narrow streets that are cooler when the houses on one side are shaded by the facades of those on the other. In one magical moment you are in Toledo, Spain, winding down a narrow cobbled street graced by tall colonial mansions rising majestically on each side, identified only by their old Castilian family coat of arms.

In the 1860s, when the massive city walls were torn down, the original compact city became Habana Vieja. Habana Vieja, even with neglect, is one of the best-preserved and harmonious colonial capitals of Spanish America. It presents a montage of urban uses, all in relative scale with each other and in quiet harmony with their shared neighborhoods.

Patina and texture are important dividends of traditional architecture. Whereas modernist buildings are often arrogant in their plain, flat, white surfaces, the Spanish colonial architecture of Habana Vieja is natural and harmonious in its dappling of architectural details, sun, and shade.

Plaza de Armas—the fence of the Castillo de la Real Fuerza and
the Palacio del Segundo Cabo beyond.

The homogenized streetscape seems to have a unique sense of grace and charm. Its buildings, streets, and plazas share a turbulent history that has made them seem to be "family," unchanged and unchallenged by modernity. Friendly neighbors on the same street, side by side, a strange mixture consisting of mansions, foreign embassies, steam laundries, tenements, warehouses, tobacco factories, schools, government offices, churches, and convents—these blend together and form one harmonious and artistic presence. Each building is a statement in itself but with limited public assertion. The rich decoration and details reflect the character of the original owner and the building's use in its own historic time, but now the structure becomes just one piece of the mosaic when it is seen as part of the city's whole. Habana Vieja has many richly textured threads of architectural styles that, when woven together, blend into a spectacular montage of urban art.

Public Plazas

The most unusual aspect of Habana Vieja is that it did not follow the Spanish colonial town planning tradition of having just one *plaza major* (major town square). In the Spanish tradition, the *plaza major* was the original marketplace that became the spiritual and geographic heart of the colonial city. Located around the *plaza major* usually were the *iglesia* (church), the *cabildo* (town hall), and the military's administrative offices as well as those of the *civil cabildo* (government). In the center of the plaza was usually a community park, often with a grand central fountain and

Plaza de Armas. The focal point has always been a historic sculpture. Originally it was a sculpture of the Spanish king Fernando VII created by Spanish sculptor Jose Alvarez Pereira, who died before finishing his work. It was finished in 1834 by another Spanish sculptor, Antonio Sola. It was then changed to the sculpture shown here, of Carlos Manuel de Céspedes, the president in arms in the rebellion against Spain during the late 1860s.

CARLOS MANUEL DE CESPEDE

a community bandstand for concerts by the municipal band. Around this central park's periphery usually was the broad *paseo* where, particularly in the evenings, many citizens would walk or relax on the public benches and watch their neighbors saunter by; perhaps the town band would play a concert, and precious time was spent with family, friends, and neighbors. In Havana, however, this traditional pattern eroded over time. Colonial life in Habana Vieja eventually revolved around four squares, not just one. Each square had its own unique history, purpose, and character, but all during their time were the center of fiestas, markets, religious processions, pedestrian strolls, and carriage rides.

The four main squares of Habana Vieja are the Plaza de Armas (the military square), the Plaza de San Francisco (the port of commerce), the Plaza de la Catedral (the religious square), and the Plaza Vieja (the residential and commercial square).

Plaza de Armas

In 1519 the first public square laid out in Havana was the Plaza de Armas. The construction of the plaza was ordered by the Marqués de la Torre on January 28, 1773, following orders from the king of Spain. The plaza was located on the same site originally selected for this purpose more than two centuries earlier. The original design is attributed to Antonio Fernández de Trebejos. The plaza was remodeled many times, the most important changes being completed in 1834 and 1935.

This square is a beautifully landscaped garden that originally focused on a central monument of the Spanish king Ferdinand VII. The square is ringed with matched shade trees that define its garden center and enclose its space. In the eighteenth century it became a favorite place for aristocratic Habaneros to walk with friends or enjoy an elegant carriage ride. In the early evening, a *volanta* (a special Havana carriage) with one, two, or even three horses (with a driver on one) would carry the young women of Havana society to listen to the military band while amusing themselves with the day's gossip and a little old-fashioned flirtation. Surrounding and defining this typical Spanish square are the city's early historic, military, political, and social institutions, namely the Castillo de la Real Fuerza, the Palacio de los Capitanes Generales, the Palacio del Segundo Cabo, and El Templete.

The Castillo de la Real Fuerza

The Castillo de la Real Fuerza (as introduced in chapter 1) is the oldest structure in Havana and the second oldest fortress in the New World. Surrounded by a gracefully shaped, broad moat with a drawbridge giving access to the vaulted interior spaces, it was built with four typically Spanish, sharp, unadorned angular ramparts, twenty feet thick and thirty-three feet high. The first Real Fuerza was built by the

Plaza de Armas with the beautiful, tall, and vertical royal palms that are native to Cuba and are used here architecturally to mirror the tall arcade of the Palacio de los Capitanes Generales and the Palacio del Segundo Cabo beyond.

Palacio de los Capitanes Generales—second-floor gallery overlooking the patio that focuses on a central statue of Christopher Columbus by J. Cucchiari from 1862. This palace is considered one of the greatest Spanish colonial buildings of the eighteenth century. It was the first official residence of the Spanish governors (1790), the U.S. administration (1898–1902), and the Cuban presidents from 1902 until the Presidential Palace was built in 1920, and it then housed the city's mayoral offices.

orders of Governor Hernando de Soto before he sailed in May 1539 from Havana to conquer Florida.

It is said that de Soto's wife, Inéz de Bobadilla, scanned the sea daily from the fort's cylindrical lookout tower for her husband's ships to return. After four years it was reported that he had died on the banks of the Mississippi, the great river he had discovered. Inéz died just a few days after receiving the tragic news of her husband's death.

The fort's primary and initial function was to protect the city from the pirate raids that were so prevalent and destructive in the sixteenth and seventeenth centuries. Once the pirates had found that Havana was an open, unlocked treasure chest—a major port for the transportation of stolen gold and silver to Spain—it became a prime target for piracy. The French pirate Jacques de Sores burned and sacked the young Havana in 1555, an act that sharply focused the Spanish on the need to fortify the city (1538–1544). After the French, the British buccaneers Sir Francis Drake and Henry Morgan, followed by the Dutch, joined the piracy. It then became a government-sanctioned enterprise that licensed attacks on Spanish galleons and their Cuban ports.

In the intervening years, the fortress has also been used as the treasury, as the home of the public archives, and as a pottery museum.

The Palacio de los Capitanes Generales

The central architectural feature of the Plaza de Armas, the magnificent Palacio de los Capitanes Generales (1791), creates the plaza's western enclosure. It is a jewel of Spanish colonial baroque architecture, which focuses on its wonderful central patio highlighting a statue of Christopher Columbus, nestled in its center among towering royal palms. Palacio de los Capitanes Generales, one of the most important buildings in the history of Havana, is part of the urban vision of the Marqués de la Torre. He obtained the support of the Spanish king for this project, which was initiated in 1776.[5]

Governor Miguel Tacón asked engineer Manuel Pastor to remodel parts of the building, giving it, according to José María Bens Arrarte, most of the architectural quality that can be admired today. Additional improvements to the building were completed in 1860. Finally, in 1930 the Cuban architects Govantes y Cabarrocas remodeled the palace, maintaining its character while adapting it to contemporary requirements.

Spain made an early commitment to use high-quality materials in the palace's construction, since it was considered the base of the royal presence in Cuba.

Palacio del Segundo Cabo—a powerful yet invitingly soft
and shaded arcade facing the Plaza de Armas.

El Templete, Plaza de Armas—a neoclassical temple where San Cristóbal de La Habana was founded in 1599. Habaneros traditionally circle the ceiba tree (shown on the left side of the photo) for good luck, just as the woman here is doing.

Precious materials were brought from Europe: 100,000 bricks from Malaga, adorned ironwork from Bilbao, and marble from Genoa, Italy, for the floors and decorations.

This palace was used as the official residence for the Spanish governors between 1791 and 1898; then for the colonial administration and prison until the end of the Spanish colonial rule; then for the American governors from 1898 until 1902 during the American intervention; and then as the first presidential palace of the new republic from 1902 until 1920. From 1920 until 1967 it housed Havana's city hall, and now it is the City of Havana Museum.

Palacio del Segundo Cabo

The Palacio del Segundo Cabo (1770) is a harmonious neighbor to the Palacio de los Capitanes Generales, defining the northwest corner of the Plaza de Armas, next to the Castillo de la Real Fuerza. This fine late baroque building, now the Instituto Cubano del Libro (Cuban Book Institute), has a wonderful high portico on its front facade with balconies above. The portico has a series of stout stone columns, a strong horizontal cornice, and graceful arches that articulate its space. This portico acts as a transitional shaded walk between the open, sunlit public plaza and the darker, private interiors of the palace. The Palacio del Segundo Cabo was built as the *casa de correos* (post office) and in 1853 became the official residence of the Segundo Cabo (Second Lieutenant, or vice-governor). As is the case of most Spanish colonial residential architecture, this colonial building is shaded and cooled by a beautiful central court onto which the surrounding gallery and rooms open.

El Templete

On the eastern side of the Plaza de Armas, El Templete (the Temple) is a small, neoclassic Doric temple that serves as a simple and dignified civic monument to commemorate Havana's creation. Built in 1828 and shaded by a majestic ceiba tree (also known as the kapok or silk cotton tree) considered sacred by some, it was erected on the assumed site of the first city of San Cristóbal de La Habana mass and city council meeting, both held in the shade of a tree in 1519. At one time there was a tall, freestanding pilaster that marked the commemorative spot where the original tree was located. This pilaster, erected by Governor Cajigal de la Vega in 1754, was placed in front of El Templete but has since been removed to expose El Templete's classic facade. It is considered good luck to circle the ceiba tree located on the side of El Templete, and many Habaneros still do so. Inside El Templete are three large paintings by the French painter Jean-Baptiste Vermay commemorating the founding of Havana. The bones of Christopher Columbus were brought to this site in 1795 to be declared genuine relics by the church.

Enclosing the east side along with El Templete is the former residence of Conde de Santovenia, Palacio del Conde Santovenia (now the Hotel Santa Isabel), a colonial mansion built in the eighteenth century. Also in the neighborhood is Casa del Árabe, a wonderful example of colonial court-garden architecture where the city's first school was housed in the seventeenth century. One block away is the Casa de la Obra Pía, a most charming and typical seventeenth-century mansion (discussed in more detail in chapter 5).

Plaza de San Francisco

During the colonial period, the port of Havana was a beehive of activity, with Spanish galleons loading treasures wrested from Spain's distant colonies, particularly Peru and Mexico, for their homeward journey. The port area was full of dockyards, moorings, wharfs, jetties, quays, warehouses, supply stores, saloons, and sailors. This was also the home of the Plaza de San Francisco, Havana's main plaza until Plaza Nueva (later Plaza Vieja) was constructed in the eighteenth century.

The Iglesia y Convento de San Francisco de Asís (1730) defines the southern boundary of the plaza and in its time was the most fashionable church in Havana, boasting that its bell tower was the highest in the city. The Franciscan monks, whose convent this was, were one of the first monastic orders to arrive in Cuba. The British used the church for Protestant worship during their brief occupation of Havana in 1762, and, as a result, it was never used afterward for Catholic services, becoming a military warehouse.[6]

A restoration of the church was completed in 1994, and the interior has been drastically simplified; however, the view from the tower is still impressive, and the crypts containing the remains of some of Havana's most powerful families are still available for viewing. In the center of the plaza stands the Fuente de los Leones (Fountain of the Lions) built by Giuseppe Gaggini in 1836, an awkward replica of the beautifully proportioned Fountain of the Lions in the main court of the Moors' Alhambra Palace in Granada, Spain.

Plaza de la Catedral

The Plaza de la Catedral is the home of the baroque Catedral de la Virgen María de la Inmaculada Concepción, commonly referred to as the Catedral San Cristóbal de La Habana or simply Catedral Colón (Columbus Cathedral). The cathedral was begun by the Jesuits in 1748, becoming a cathedral in 1777, ten years after Carlos III banned the Jesuits from Cuba. On January 15, 1796, Christopher Columbus's remains were brought to Cuba from Santo Domingo, where they rested in the

Iglesia y Convento de San Francisco de Asís (1730), Plaza de San Francisco. The bell tower of the church is the focal point around which the plaza revolves (ca. 1900).

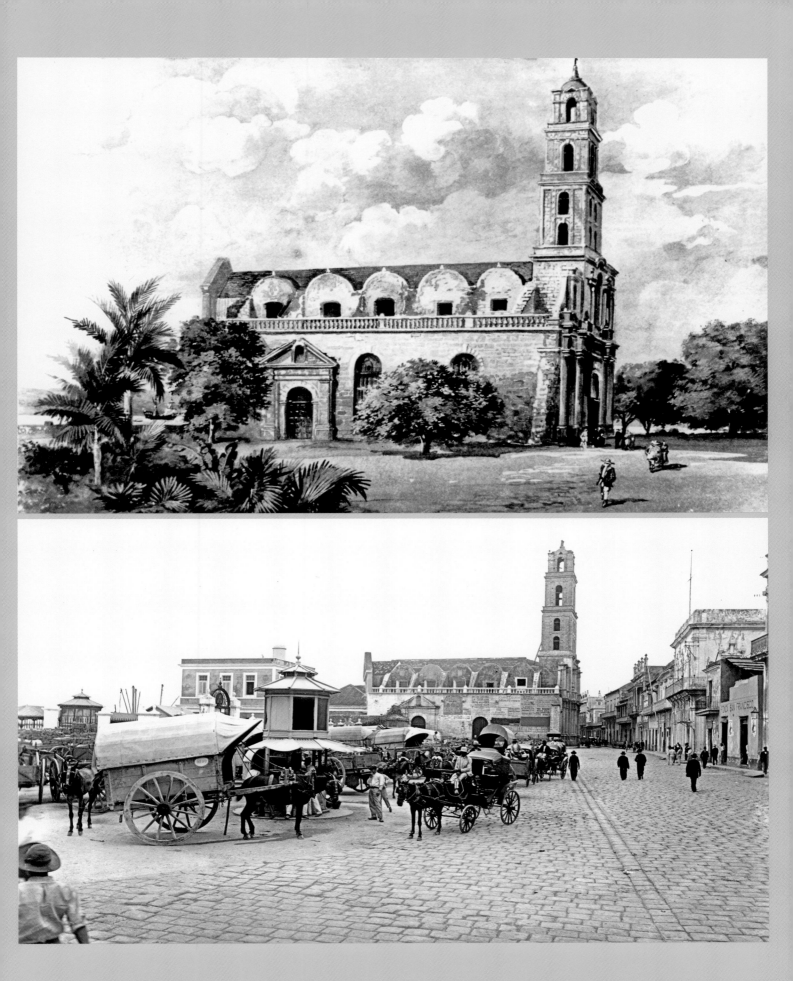

Plaza Vieja—as seen from the balcony of the Casa de los Condes de Jaruco—being restored in 1997.

Plaza Vieja as seen through a *mediopunto* (stained glass) window of Casa de los Condes de Jaruco.

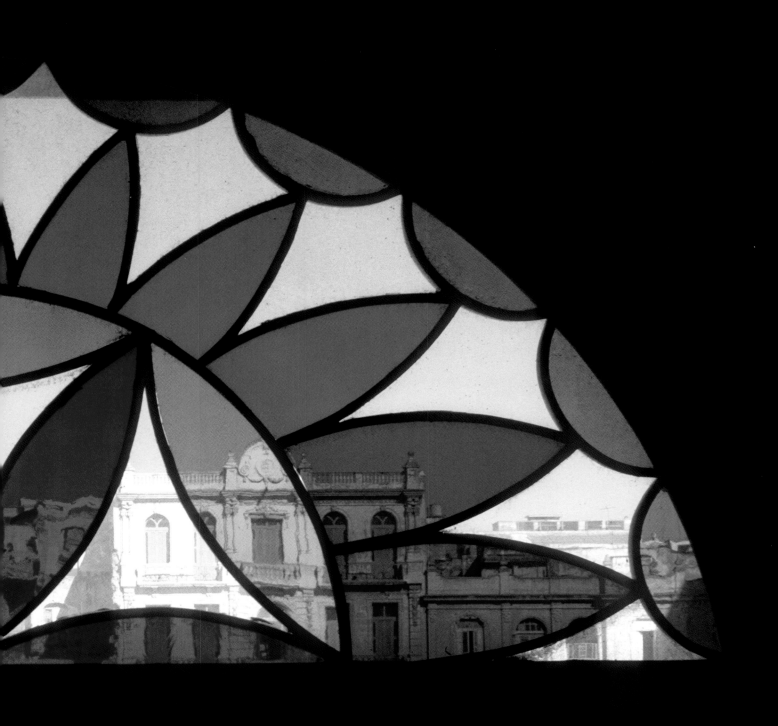

Catedral San Cristóbal until 1899, when they were transferred to Seville's cathedral after the Spanish-American War and Spain's loss of Cuba.

Spanish colonial churches, with their Mudejar (Moorish) facade, are derived from the Spanish regional styles contemporary with the colonial period such as those found in the former Reino de Sevilla, the modern Spanish provinces of Seville, Huelva, Cádiz, and part of Malaga.[7] This cathedral has a relatively simple stone facade that conceals the wealth of beautiful vestments and old silver contained within its ancient walls. Although the historic facade remains, the church's interior was remodeled in the classical style in 1814.

This harmonious plaza is graced by fine examples of early colonnaded, domestic mansions from the eighteenth century that once were the domain of the high nobility of Habana Vieja. The Seminario de San Carlos y San Ambrosio was built by the Jesuits behind the cathedral as an annex. It is an example of an austere sixteenth-century Spanish architecture, with an entrance of similar proportions and details as the central Mudéjar facade of the Catedral San Cristóbal de La Habana. The seminary's interior rooms open to a large, classic Spanish patio and garden, creating a traditional, spiritual, contemplation space, cloistered by a colonnaded walk and galleries.

Plaza Vieja

The last plaza in Habana Vieja is Plaza Vieja (Old Plaza, 1559), originally called Plaza Nueva (New Square). Plaza Vieja is surrounded by arcaded colonial buildings—important mansions and palaces built over four centuries. After the Plaza de Armas diminished in importance, this square became the political, social, and commercial center of Havana, where the city's high society lived and where foreign dignitaries visited. In the nineteenth century, after the Plaza de Armas was again improved and other public places created, this plaza was renamed Plaza Vieja.

Originally its stately mansions offered wonderful views of the square through their second-floor *mediopunto* windows (windows with stained-glass fanlights and/or side-lights). This colored glass—a distinctive Cuban folk art introduced in the mid-eighteenth century—filtered the harsh tropical sun while dazzling the inhabitants with a constantly evolving kaleidoscope of brilliant colors cascading over their mansion's walls and floors.

The arcades around the plaza would often be draped by billowing cloths hung between the columns to create much-appreciated shade. This arcade was a wonderful place to walk along, particularly when the afternoon sun cast distinctive patterns of long shadows and light deep into the arcade, outlining its parade of columns.

Colonnaded palaces define and enclose the Plaza Vieja, the residence for former Havana socialites, titled aristocrats, and foreign dignitaries during four centuries.

Governor Miguel Tacón, Marqués de la Union de Cuba (1834–1838)

The Marqués de la Torre completed many other initiatives, but it was Governor General Miguel Tacón y Rosique, Marqués de la Union de Cuba (1834–1838), who continued the improvement of Havana and implemented most of the changes that upgraded the city in the nineteenth century.

Two important architectural edifices were completed during this period. The first was El Templete, designed by the Cuban architect Antonio Maria de la Torre. It is considered a landmark because it introduced neoclassicism to the Cuban architectural vocabulary upon its completion in 1828. Another project that introduced a monumental neoromantic style was the Portada (portal) to El Cementerio de Colón (Columbus Cemetery), designed by architect Calixto de Loira between 1871 and 1886. These two projects were landmarks in the historic development of Cuban architecture.

Governor Tacón ordered the redevelopment of the Avenida San Luis Gonzaga (later named De la Reina) and, as a continuation, built Paseo Militar o de Tacón, the city's most important boulevard. It was decorated with fountains and statues.

At the end of Paseo del Prado, Tacón ordered the construction of a summer residence for the governors, to be called La Quinta de los Molinos. It has been remodeled several times since, and today it is a museum with extensive tropical gardens (see chapter 11).

After Tacón, other governors implemented improvements in the city, but the most important was the demolishing of the walls, initiated on August 8, 1863, under the government of General Domingo Dulce. One hundred twenty-three years after their construction, the walls had never been used in the defense of the city. The city walls represented a physical barrier between the two parts of Havana, Habana Vieja and the newly emerging Central Habana. The demolition of these walls was the first emblematic step in the development of Central Habana. The Reparto de las Murallas, the linear area that had been occupied by the walls of the city, was an urban landmark recognized by UNESCO as a monument to humanity.

Preceding pages: Plaza Vieja—originally called Plaza Nueva (New Square) when it was conceived in 1559 as a large public square and center of commerce. A quick glance at this contemporary photograph of this two-story corner arcaded building shows the extent of the plaza's disintegration. After years of total neglect, exacerbated by tropical heat and humidity, the walls, shutter doors, exposed overhang, and soffits are in a state of advanced decay. The glass transoms are broken, opening the interiors to further elements of dissipation.

Outside the original city walls at the Puerta de Monserrate, aristocratic Habaneros stroll
and take a carriage ride to enjoy the fresh country air beyond the confined Habana Vieja,
before the city walls were demolished in 1863.

José Martí sculpture, Parque Central, sculpted in Carrara marble by José Vilalta de Saavedra (1905). In the late nineteenth century, José Martí, Cuba's national hero, called for the end to the Spanish colonial system and the establishment of a Cuban republican government. Martí was popular not only in Cuba but throughout Latin America as a poet, journalist, writer, and essayist.

Chapter 3

From Walled Colonial City to the Capital of the Republic (1864–1898)

European Urbanism Came to Havana: Governor Felipe Fondesuiela, Marqués de la Torre (1771–1776)

Detail, pedestal of the José Martí sculpture, memorial to the Spanish-American War, Parque Central.

The Spanish-American War (1898)

In the first quarter of the nineteenth century, Cuba's population exploded as the African slave trade and the island's numbers of free blacks continued to expand. By 1825 Spain's colonies in Latin America had won their independence, except for Cuba and Puerto Rico.

The considerable growth of the sugar industry at this time had changed the social structure of Cuba. During the brief English occupation, Havana was opened to trade with England and its North American colonies and prospered. In the years after the occupation, the sugar industry grew, with annual production increasing from 14,000 tons in 1790 to 34,000 tons in 1805. During the nineteenth century, sugar and coffee became increasingly important to the economy. Since these crops needed less land than the raising of cattle, the large cattle estates were broken up into smaller sections, which were sold for sugar or coffee cultivation. Then, in the 1840s, coffee prices fell, and capital and labor flowed into growing sugarcane. By 1860 there were 2,000 sugar mills, and a new class of rural proprietors had emerged. Coupled with the railroad coming to Cuba to transport cane from the fields to the mills and docks of Havana, this created a great surge of wealth in Havana. Afraid of a weakened Spain and the possibility of slave rebellion, the new aristocracy looked to the United States for a more permanent and protective relationship.

By 1825 Spain's colonies in Latin America had won their independence, except Cuba and Puerto Rico. The overseers of Cuba's slave society were kept in a constant state of terror after the slave rebellion in Haiti in the 1790s, where Napoleon's army of 20,000 men had been defeated by a new black republic.

This was a time of Havana's flourishing urban development. Insulated and confined behind its massive city walls, Havana became a beautiful colonial city, filled with sculptural forts, public plazas, and wonderful residential architecture. But that was about to change, as were the city's history, culture, and urban development.

In 1868 the first war for independence began when Carlos Manuel de Céspedes freed his slaves and called for emancipation and independence. This first war, which cost 250,000 Cuban lives, raged for a decade, ending in 1878. In 1886 slavery was abolished, and American investments in the Cuban sugar industry surged.

The second half of the nineteenth century was a period of dramatic changes in Cuba and its capital city. On October 10, 1868, Cubans, dominated until then by the Spanish government, wrote a "Declaration of Independence" and started what was later called the Ten Years' War. That year the first Cuban constitution was also written and adopted by the insurgents. This constitution proclaimed independence from Spain and the creation of a new Republic of Cuba. In 1878 Spain signed a peace treaty with the Cubans; however, this was a temporary peace, followed by La Guerra Chiquita (the Little War) from 1879 to 1880.

José Martí, a lawyer, writer, and poet, led the new War of Independence. After being imprisoned for his anti-Spanish writings, Martí was deported to Spain, and he moved to the United States in 1881. In 1892 Marti founded the Cuban Revolutionary Party, with Máximo Gómez as supreme commander. They landed a revolutionary party in 1895 on Cuba's southeastern coast near Cajobabo, and started the War of Independence. On May 19, 1895, Martí was shot to death in the first battle when he rode headlong into enemy lines.

In the United States, war hysteria was whipped up by the newspapers of William Randolph Hearst and Joseph Pulitzer with tales of Spanish atrocities. On February 15, 1898, the USS *Maine*, a battleship, was sunk in Havana harbor with the loss of 260 lives, and "Remember the Maine" became the battle cry in the States for the Spanish-American War.

On April 25, 1898, the United States declared war on Spain, and the war was fought both on land and at sea—first with American ships off Santiago, Cuba, bottling up the Spanish navy, and then on land with the famous Battle of San Juan Hill, where Teddy Roosevelt is said to have led the cavalry charge of his Rough Riders. The victorious American troops sustained 1,400 casualties. Two days later the Spanish fleet tried to break the American blockade and in several hours was completely defeated. The United States won the war and took possession of Cuba, Puerto Rico, Guam, and the Philippine Islands, the last of the Spanish Empire. Peace arrived with the signing of the Treaty of Paris between Spain and the United States. The Cuban war heroes were often ignored after the war despite their years of struggle against Spain and the thousands of lives that criollos gave for their country. Most of this war was fought outside Havana, so the urban life of the Habaneros continued almost undisturbed.

The Plan for Central Habana (Ensanche)

The rural land beyond the glacis (the sloping ground forming a military setback from the wall for defensive purposes), enforced by the Spanish army, was experiencing a population explosion. More than 40,000 residents settled in this region at the beginning of the nineteenth century, a population larger than those living within the original city walls.

The Spanish authorities destroyed this slum periodically, but they never controlled it. This situation changed when Spain adopted the Royal Ordinances for

Detail, pedestal of the José Martí sculpture, memorial to the Spanish-American War, Parque Central. This animated sculptural detail tries, with the sculptor's chisel, to capture the spirit of the Cuban War of Independence. Public parks need monuments plus the elements of parkscape such as benches, walks, and shade trees to give them character, interest, and relevance.

the Expansion of the Spanish Cities in 1817. Havana decided to implement the Ley de Ensanches (new ordinances for expansion), and in January 1819 the municipal government adopted an urban plan for the area outside the walls. This was the first urban plan for Havana since Cristóbal de Roda's original plan in 1603.

Designed by the engineer Antonio Maria de la Torre and enthusiastically implemented, the plan was similar to Barcelona's *Eixample* (expansion) designed by Ildefons Cerdà after the demolition of that city's walls. One member of the city council was assigned full time to supervise the implementation of the proposals. Under his supervision, members of the Spanish army marked the ground at every corner of every block as well as marking property lines. In less than ten years the area was transformed from a slum to an important urbanized part of the city.

De la Torre's plan defined the western edge of Paseo de Isabel II (Paseo del Prado), facilitating the future redesign of the area. The coast was the northern boundary of the Ensanche, where the waterfront was used for recreation, and humble bath cabins were built in the back patios of the houses fronting on the final street, Ancha del Norte (today, San Lazaro Street).

The southern limit of the Ensanche was the Avenida de la Reina (today, Avenida Simon Bolivar). This avenue was extended by Governor Miguel Tacón when he ordered the construction of Paseo Militar o de Tacón from the end of Reina to the edge of El Príncipe Castle.

The eastern boundary of the project was Belascoain Street. This area was under development pressures because Havana was growing in this direction, and De la Torre's urban design principles for the Ensanche were ignored, resulting in a confusing urban pattern that is still a problem for Havana today.

Reparto de las Murallas

The demolition of Havana's city walls was authorized by the queen of Spain on June 11, 1863, and the work officially started in August of that year. Although it took many years to complete, the entire project started the new growth of the city, for the urbanizing of the former wall area was initiated immediately and successfully completed just two years later. It provided the resources for new urban growth.

The adopted plan, the Reparto de las Murallas (the plan for the Murallas neighborhood—*reparto* is a land division), was designed by the engineer/architect Juan Bautista Orduña. The plan had two important components. The first was the extension of Paseo del Prado to the edge of the Arsenal (military depot), creating a monumental main street for Havana. This was rejected because of its high cost. The second, and presumably more affordable, proposal was the construction of two parallel avenues along the former site of the walls. These two avenues—Zulueta (Calle

4011. Indian Park, Havana, Cuba.

HABANA. Fuente de la India.
India Monument

Fuente de la India Noble Habana (1837)—a fountain crowned by a serene, elegant statue of the queen after whom the province of La Habana was named. The fountain is a symbol of Havana and has been relocated within the city several times. It now resides in Parque de la Fraternidad, facing El Capitolio Nacional.

Agramonte) and Monserrate (Avenida de Bélgica)—were built as important parts of the Reparto de las Murallas.

The Cuban architect José María Bens Arrarte, a respected historian, called the demolition of the walls and the construction of the Reparto de las Murallas the great adventure of Havana from the middle of the nineteenth century to the beginning of the twentieth century.

An Aristocratic City

During the eighteenth and nineteenth centuries, when the late afternoon sun projected its golden beams across the pastel facades of Havana's palaces and mansions, the aristocratic Habaneros would view their city from high on their balconies with a certain amount of pride. These Spanish colonial officials, affluent merchants, and plantation owners had transformed Havana into a city of wealth and sophistication.

Plazuela de Albear. Aristocratic women in the latest fashion, with large, elegant hats and parasols at their sides, grace this charming, human-scale urban square, which centers on the monument to Francisco de Albear, engineer for Havana's waterworks (1870). Note also in this slice out of the past the cloths shading the arcade behind (ca. 1900).

Havana has developed through the years with a peppering of eclectic architectural facades, making the city a living three-dimensional architectural history book. Its Romanesque, Renaissance, baroque, rococo, neoclassical, Spanish colonial, and Moorish architecture is seamlessly blended with late-nineteenth-century Art Nouveau, early-twentieth-century Art Deco, and the modernist International Style. However, Havana's true expression of its exotic and aristocratic culture is found in its Spanish colonial architecture, rooted in its centuries-old Iberian and African traditions. This is an aristocratic architecture of elegant palm-filled patios, gentle fountains, and ornate iron balconies, complementing an eloquent culture epitomized by an erudite carriage ride on the elegant *volanta* (carriage).

Of the aristocrats of Havana's society, those born in Spain considered themselves superior to the others, while the next social level was anyone of high birth but born in Cuba. Although Spain was the aristocrats' mother country during the eighteenth and nineteenth centuries, France was the fashion and cultural center of the world, and Havana's elite dressed and danced like the French. There was a major French immigration from French Louisiana as well as Haiti and Santo Domingo after slave insurrections.

The Streets of Havana

During Havana's turbulent history, its streets were a crazy quilt of activity, where the middle and lower classes played out their daily lives. Havana's warehouses were brimming with the wealth plundered from Mexico and Peru plus luxuries and delicacies imported from throughout the world. The city hummed with the life of casinos, cafés, bars, markets, offices, and shops, the finest of these lining Calles Obispo and O'Reilly. The streets were full of servants and slaves, blacks and mulattos, vendors and fishermen, peasants from the countryside, sailors and soldiers, gamblers with cards and dice, carriage drivers on *volantas*, and merchants and traders from distant lands.

Havana's streets, from dusk to dawn, were stages on which all the Habaneros could perform their urban magic. Havana was contradictory: sophisticated and common, elegant and noisy, witty and arrogant, beautiful and plain, spacious and narrow. Entertainment on the streets, which were often shaded from above with billowing cloth and awnings (*toldos*) to soften the harsh sun, consisted of religious processions, parades, celebrations, fiestas, contests, markets, proclamations, fistfights, bullfights, cockfights, bazaars, circuses, dances, and retreats, or simply an evening with a musical group in a town square.[1]

Viewing this exciting, if not ignoble, scene were the women of society standing high on their mansions' private balances or peeking from their partially hidden

position behind their *persianas* (jalousies), doors, or windows. They were the voluptuous women of society, always dressed in fine, glistening, imported silk with low-cut, revealing dresses and holding beautifully painted Spanish fans. During the 1880s, these aristocrats could escape the dense urban confines of Habana Vieja and stretch their legs in the new open spaces of the emerging Central Habana and the Prado.

The Culture of the *Volantas*

The fine gentlemen of Havana, dressed by their slave valets in black frock coats, white linen shirts, silk cravats, and fine hats, would stroll the streets with little care while their ladies would stay in their mansions, visit friends, or ride high in their *carruajes* (carriages)—the cultural icon called *volantas*. At one time there were 3,000 of these elegant *volantas* in Havana.[2] The *volantas* were special, consisting of two giant red rear wheels with black trim; a leather-hooded cabin for privacy and sun protection; silver footrests; and a Persian carpet—all suspended on leather straps between two long, gracefully curved poles. The *volanta* was driven by a *calesero*, a black man of relatively high position, with a stunning, perfectly groomed stallion. Since the fine ladies of Havana's colonial society wore delicate silk shoes, they would seldom venture onto the street and then only in pairs. They would order their *volanta* and enter directly from their grand staircase in full fashion. They would then be taken for a comfortable ride or to their favorite pastime—to shop at a fine shop and perhaps buy an imported and enormously broad feathered hat. Once at the shop they would not descend the *volanta*, but would have the hat brought to them in the carriage, and then they would be driven home.[3]

The *calesero*, using his long leather whip, would drive in striking fashion through Habana Vieja's narrow streets, wearing a velvet jacket, lace shirt, white waistcoat, breeches, tall leather boots, and a silk top hat. Before the city walls were removed in the 1860s, it was fashionable to take a *volanta* ride outside the confines of the walled city to enjoy the country air and show off your *volanta* and perhaps your

Preceding pages: The facades of present-day Havana are not pure architecture of stone; rather, they are extensions of the streets—alive with large openings, billowing curtains, blaring radios, ornate balconies, and Habaneros enjoying the fresh air and the lively street scene below. This typical scene is an example of the marriage of Havana's architecture and the culture of Cuba.

Right: Casa de Santiago C. Burnham, Habana Vieja. The *mediopunto* (stained glass), set as the window's fanlights and side-lights, add that special Cuban sparkle to Havana's Spanish colonial homes in a union of art, architecture, and culture. The feeling created is one of tropical lightness and spontaneity (1817).

eligible daughter.[4] In the 1880s, with the building of the Teatro Tacón and the widening of the Prado, which became Paseo Extramural, *a paseo en carruaje* (a passage for carriages), aristocrats would enjoy riding up and down the Prado between the waterfront and Parque Central.[5]

The Language of the Fan

In aristocratic Spain and Havana, a cool breeze often was choreographed by a fashionable and elaborately decorated hand-painted fan. The "Spanish language of the fan" was a way for high society to communicate the messages of amour in a subtle but not too secretive way. The language of the fan is now a forgotten language, but in Havana in the eighteenth and nineteenth centuries, it was understood and used.

Here are some examples a woman might use:

- Showing up briefly on the balcony, slowly fanning herself, and returning inside, shutting the balcony door: I can't go out.

- Appearing briefly on the balcony, excitedly fanning herself, and quickly going inside, leaving the balcony door open: I'll go out soon.

- Quickly fanning herself: I love you so much.

- Passing the fan from hand to hand: I see you are looking at another woman.

- Quickly and impetuously closing the fan: I'm jealous.

- Resting the fan on her heart: My love for you is breaking my heart.

- Fanning herself with her left hand: Don't flirt with that woman.[6]

Left: Plaza Vieja—arcade and *volanta* (carriage). The billowing white cloths create shade while providing a magical, wavelike rhythm, a good example of the simple and natural way of controlling the harsh, hot tropical environment.

Following pages: Palacio de los Capitanes Generales, the Salón of the Town Council. High ceilings, crystal chandeliers, decorative wainscot, fine furniture, statuary, fine porcelains, a grand piano, regal portraits, and Persian carpets all add to the creation of a refined and stylish interior—the perfect example of the elegant lifestyle of aristocratic Havana.

Parque de la Libertad de Matanzas, aristocratic *carruaje* (carriage)—a Cuban cultural icon called the *volanta*. The *volanta* was usually a one-horse leather carriage sitting on two enormous wheels. It was driven by a postilion—known as a *calesero*—usually in proper dress and high boots (ca. 1900).

Chapter 4

Havana at the Turn of the Twentieth Century (1898–1902)

Glorieta de la Punta (bandstand at the point of the Entrance Canal), at the beginning of the Malecón with the Canal de Entrada and Castillo del Morro beyond, 1904. Here is Havana's nineteenth-century aristocratic city on display. It's a beautiful sunny afternoon with the Habaneros dressed in their finest: men in suits and hats, women in full dresses with large and stylish hats. The *volantas* (carriages) are on parade, and the band is playing in the Glorieta de la Punta, a circular temple built in 1902 to commemorate the students assassinated by the Spaniards in 1871.

El Capitolio Nacional—the capitol of the new republic. This building, with its dome, is not only a symbol of the city and the new republic, but it is also an example of important civic architecture harmonizing and enriching a neighborhood and a city. This is the opposite of the contemporary fashion of celebrity architecture, which is boastful and either ignores or dominates its urban environment (1929).

AS THE WORLD CHURNED with startling changes during the last half of the nineteenth century, Havana stayed basically stable and maintained its own urban character not affected by modernity. It is important to understand the essence of what was happening in the world at the time to understand and appreciate the lack of urban change in Havana during the fifty-year period prior to the turn of the century.

The last half of the nineteenth century was a transitional time in Western history, a period of intense innovation in most fields of human endeavor. At a time when the world's "aristocracy" lost most of their power, world society changed in fundamental ways with the beginning of the Industrial Revolution and the age of creative innovation, technical progress, and rapid growth of cities.

At the same time, the nineteenth century experienced an explosion in the use of new architectural materials and engineering skills: the imaginative use of cast iron, then the development of the steel frame and the elevator, which together gave rise to the skyscraper; the extensive use of glass, as used in the Crystal Palace at the Universal Exhibition in Paris (1855); and the rediscovery of the plastic building material ferroconcrete. All of these created profound changes in the architectural world—except in Havana, which continued in its traditional historic mode.

Charles Darwin rewrote the prehistory of the world, while the steam engine and railroads increased the speed of travel and reduced the size of the world. Steam-powered barges cleaned Havana Bay. The new railroads, for which Cuba was the fifth country in the world and the first Spanish-speaking country to use, permitted the expansion of sugarcane planting since the cane could now be transported quickly from the Bejucal valley without losing its sugar content while waiting for a horse cart to transport it to the mills and warehouses of Havana. These railroads, therefore, compressed time and space in the production of sugar and added greatly to the wealth of Havana.[1]

As the century progressed, nationalism gained ground as the common people became self-aware of their potential power and rode the wave of revolution—political, military, and artistic. New concepts not only changed the lives of the people but also the cities in which they lived. Claims for national independence and human rights began to ripple through Europe and eventually through the New World colonies.

Independence became the rallying cry throughout Spanish America and finally spread to Spain's last bastion—Cuba. It was a time of ferment and change, creating an atmosphere for new concepts in city development; a new order was emerging.[2]

4015. Presidents Palace and Senate Building, Havana.

Plaza de Armas. The Palace de los Capitanes Generales after independence became the Presidential Palace, the first home of the presidents of the new republic.

Havana, a traditional city, did not seem to be affected at this time by the worldwide cultural revolution and the birth of modernity.

However, in Havana, the turn of the twentieth century was in some ways a traumatic time. During the nineteenth century, Havana was, for the ruling class, a city of European elegance and excesses tempered only by the tropical heat and humidity. Havana was the last dazzling center of the diminishing Spanish Empire. This century finally brought to an end this long colonial period, where the Spanish aristocracy lived a palatial life in palatial mansions in a palatial city, a lifestyle held high on the backs of slaves and the wealth of white gold—sugar.

The approach of the new century, the fin de siècle era, saw the city of Havana in the throes of three revolutions: first, an urban revolution with the taking down of the city walls by Spanish real estate interests in 1863; second, the social revolution with the abolition of slavery in 1886; and third, the successful War of Independence during 1895–1898.

Avenida de las Misiones—in front of the Presidential Palace, now Museum of the Revolution, between Zulueta and Monserrate avenues. The landscape of this avenue was designed by Jean Claude Nicolas Forestier, the international city planner, urbanologist, and landscape architect who designed much of early-twentieth-century Havana. In the original plan, the avenue was to end in monumental stairs reaching the oceanfront, but the plan had to be modified because of the topography.

Sala del Cabildo of Havana (Hall of the Town Council), Palacio de los Capitanes Generales, Plaza de Armas. As the nineteenth century ended, the old Spanish aristocracy lost their position and power and gave way to a new wealthy class, created mainly on the prosperity of sugar, coffee, tobacco, immigration, land speculation, and the importance of Havana as a commercial port and shipbuilding center.

At the dawn of the twentieth century, architects were rebelling from their reflections of the historic past and the grand costumes of the faded cultures and cities. In the decade before the turn of the century, Havana experienced some of the same dichotomies of the academic traditionalist versus the rebel in its architectural and artistic endeavors.

As the twentieth century began, Cuba and its capital, Havana, enjoyed a wave of prosperity primarily due to the wealth created by the prospering sugar industry, coffee cultivation, land speculation, and the creation of new neighborhoods (the *reparto*) as Havana expanded it borders. The old order was dying, and a new society of Creole hacendados and entrepreneurs rose to enjoy the good life of Havana. Havana was becoming a modern city, and it looked to other societies as models for its urban growth and form.

Fanned by massive immigration from Spain and the American paternal drive for the Americanization of the new democracy during the three years of occupation by the United States (1899–1902), Havana gained a status previously unknown. The strong flames of change, fanned by the nationalistic pride born with the independence of the new republic, made Havana a potential future star among America's new constellations.

Under American Intervention (1899–1902)

The United States took control of Cuba from Spain on January 1, 1899, under the direction of General John R. Brooke. Eleven months later, in December 1899, General Dr. Leonard Wood was designated military governor of Cuba. Wood initiated an intense program of public health, directed by Dr. William C. Gorgas, that improved the general living conditions in the entire country.

In Havana, Wood improved the water supply, drainage, and sewer system, and started regular garbage collection and the paving of streets—completing an excellent public infrastructure in a short period of time. Another accomplishment of the Wood administration was the development and implementation of a national educational plan that included new curriculum, text books, teacher training, school construction at all levels, and new laws regulating public and private education. This extraordinary program was guided by the American educator Alexis E. Fryer, with the active participation of Cuban educators.

Wood also dictated the separation of church and state, facilitated the preparation of a new constitution, and at the same time acted as a catalyst for the massive American investment that overnight gained control of the weak Cuban economy. The American intervention established an unusual governmental structure born out of the emergency of the time. It was a government defined by its military struc-

Top: Sevilla Biltmore Hotel—Spanish patio with its focal point, the typical embellished wall fountain, a place for women to have tea. Adding to the festive, tropical feeling are potted palms, Andalusian tile, and a richly ornamental recessed upper gallery. Paseo del Prado, Havana (1919).

Above: Plaza de Armas. The Palacio del Segundo Cabo became the Senate Building. This civic square is still relevant today, as it has been for centuries. It is well defined by its surrounding historic buildings and well patterned and articulated with fine landscape. Public plazas are a legacy of Spanish urban planning that unfortunately have been left out of the contemporary urban vocabulary of the United States with few exceptions, such as the squares of Savannah, Georgia.

ture and power but also one that worked in close harmony with the most responsible and educated Cuban citizenry

The leadership of Governor Wood facilitated the successful transition to the first democratically elected government, presided over by Don Tomás Estrada-Palma.

Architecture and Urbanism during the Transition from Colony to New Republic

The urban vision for the capital of the new republic was conceived by architect and professor Pedro Martínez Inclán in *La Habana Actual* (Havana Today, published in 1925) and the Ordenanzas de Construcción for the Reparto de las Murallas, which were officially published in a map of the area in 1861. At that time Spanish control of Cuba was being confronted by increasing unrest, culminating in the Cuban wars of independence of 1868–1878 and 1895–1898, which preceded the Spanish-American War that ended the Spanish rule of Cuba in 1899.

In spite of these political conditions, the availability of developable land in the new center of Havana attracted the interest of wealthy Spanish and Cuban families anxious to show their confidence and support for the Cuban government while at the same time exerting the power of their new wealth. The two groups provided the initial capital for the urban growth of the city, developing neighborhood projects that today are part of Havana's architectural heritage. The Reparto de las Murallas was like a bridge between two political systems, allowing the continuity of colonial urban traditions and at the same time making it easier to implement the necessary changes to be introduced by the new republic.

At this time the participatory involvement of a large part of the city's population began to be felt in the city's development. Architecture improved with the availability of qualified contractors and the opening of professional schools training architects, engineers, and construction workers. Combined with considerable immigration of trained construction supervisors from Spain, particularly from Barcelona, these new contractors brought many styles and architectural excellence to the emerging new neighborhoods of Havana.

The land made available with the taking down of the city's walls and the opening of other areas that were formally under the military's control, particularly the coastal areas, became a fertile ground for new architecture and growth. Urban renewal started in the city, and new developments began being built in the areas now opened for urban expansion. This urban growth did not destroy the original character of the city but was assimilated into its fabric and retained the essence of its urban quality.

The new city emerged with wide boulevards, promenades, and streets lined with beautiful buildings, rich with details, galleries, and arcades. In this emerging Havana there was no separation of uses, but a mixed-use city appeared with housing, hotels, theaters, recreation, light industry, and business all as sympathetic neighbors.

Today, Havana is a city of 2.3 million residents, the center of political and social life in Cuba. The city's oceanfront is the best known and admired area with avenues, plazas, and architectural monuments of unique quality that have created an urban landscape and seascape that attract admirers from all parts of the world.

Behind this edge of Las Murallas, which was largely developed following urban ordinances (from the ones by Alonso de Cáceres in 1574 up to the one adopted in 1861 and implemented before the twentieth century), was a large area urbanized by land owners, land speculators, and developers who, according to architect and historian José María Bens Arrarte, were guided by a policy of indifference and tolerance (*dejar hacer*), creating a fragmented urban pattern that was in sharp contrast to the more orderly development of the coastal area of Havana.

❈ *Part II*

Havana's Architecture and Urban Landscape

Chapter 5

Spanish Colonial Architecture

Casa de la Obra Pía. The arched openings that surround the balcony
frame the views of the interior Spanish court.

The Spanish Colonial House: In Praise of the Enclosed Space

Habana Vieja hosts the wonders of Spanish colonial architecture: an architecture that both historically and environmentally was perfectly adaptable for Havana's location and climate. Two of the primary environmental factors of Cuba are its intense heat and strong, topical sun. The architectural answer was found in the wide use of patios, porticos, and *persianas* (adjustable louvers on doors or windows) that brought welcomed fresh air and shade, particularly before the advent of modern air-conditioning.

Habana Vieja's street facades often are quite plain, a characteristic of Moorish and Spanish Andalusian architecture. Moorish culture exudes modesty and has a bias for interior orientation as opposed to an exuberant street presence. Islamic architecture and its derivative, Spanish colonial architecture, are a "hidden architecture," where the facade does not give an indication of the building's inner organization or purpose.[1] In Habana Vieja, facades usually have large, barred, rectangular windows and occasionally ornate doorways, which, when open, reveal the beautiful patios and gardens beyond. The buildings are usually smoothly plastered and gaily colored in startling combinations that astonish the eye and, when set against the clear blue tropical sky, constitute no small portion of the charm of Havana.

Habana Vieja's typical colonial mansion, constructed primarily on two floors, particularly of the seventeenth and eighteenth centuries, has a facade that covers the *portales* (public walk) with iron-railed balconies opening to the street below. The ground floor was devoted to commerce, either shops or warehouses for the business of the residence's owner. The main floor, accessible by a wide and often graciously winding staircase, was the primary living quarters for the family. Here there were a series of large, airy rooms and salons connected by a continuous open but covered gallery. This gallery, consisting of a series of graceful arches, acts as a shady link creating a harmonious transition between the interior and exterior spaces. The family rooms and salons open to this gallery either by pairs of full-length doors or windows protected by turned wooden *rejas* (grills) and also by *persianas* to keep out the strong sunlight. Between these two primary floors is an *entresuelo* (mezzanine), where the servants/slaves worked and lived and the family offices were housed. This entire house was wrapped around a lushly landscaped patio. Here the enclosed space is equal to, or more important than, the interior architectural spaces.

The Courtyard Patio House

Spanish residential architecture centers on interior living, as opposed to a major dedication to the exterior appearance and concern for passersby. The interior Spanish patio is alive with the sound and spray of water as it splashes from the central or wall fountain, animated by the billowing lace curtains on the surrounding balcony doors and windows. The patio is cooled when tropical breezes are created by the contrast between the bright, hot sun of the patio and its rising air and the cooler air from the shaded surrounding building that rushes in to replace it. From the patio and gallery, the air then circulates into the surrounding spacious rooms, which were generously proportioned for the large family and lavish entertainment for Havana's society. As the patio's strong tropical sunlight enters the interior rooms, it is filtered and softened by the beautiful Cuban stained-glass *mediopunto* windows, which cast bursts of soft color that brighten each room.

Spanish colonial architecture embraces the world of privacy and is perfect for the tropics, for it encourages natural ventilation while softening the effects of a strong Caribbean sun and its accompanying humidity. In Spanish colonial architecture, the interior space hides the building's principal features and uses behind a placid exterior. The interior rooms are usually absent of specific form or specific function. Each room can adapt to a variety of purposes, again in the Islamic tradition, a tradition where the building's three architectural elements—the patio, gallery, and high-ceilinged rooms—form one harmonious unity.[2]

Spanish and Mediterranean architecture since Roman times have featured the patio/court house, a house surrounding and opening to one or several interior patios. This was the prevailing architectural style in Habana Vieja. This changed when El Cerro and El Vedado neighborhoods were built in the late nineteenth and early twentieth centuries, for they adapted the American garden style of residential architecture with a grid plan of villas. This style eliminated the Spanish central courtyard and substituted the American suburban house, a design glamorized by the Anglo-Saxon concept of City Beautiful, where the houses are self-contained and often self-aggrandized entities, set back from the street and located, more or less, in the center

Opposite, top: A typical interior of a Spanish courtyard of the prestigious palaces and residences found in Habana Vieja, defined and enclosed by porticoed colonnades and galleries. The ground level is stronger and heavier, while the upper residential level offers a finer, lighter feeling.

Opposite, bottom: A typical second-level gallery arcade, which is lighter and in a more human scale than the heavier ground-level colonnade. Here the scale is personal in keeping with this level's residential use, with graceful arches and a fine, almost transparent iron rail overlooking the landscaped central patio. The gallery is a transitional space that allows the eye to relax from the brightness of the sunlit exterior and prepares one for the lower light level of the interior spaces.

Above: A grand stairway, in its present state, a typical feature of Cuban-Spanish architecture connecting in a most gracious way the generally commercial ground floor with the private residential floor above.

Preceding pages: A typical Cuban-Spanish courtyard defined by a semicircular, arcaded colonnade on the ground level and gallery above. This photo shows the *entresuelo* (mezzanine) inserted between the two principal floors, which creates the need for taller first-floor columns and a dramatic change in proportions and scale of the courtyard.

of the lot and surrounded by a garden. This suburbanized residential architecture that shows off the owner's wealth to the street and neighborhood became as popular among the affluent in burgeoning Havana as it was in the United States, particularly in the twentieth century.

The genesis of the Spanish courtyard/garden house goes back to the ancient Egyptian house with a central open court, which in turn inspired the classic Greek's Hellenistic court house, the Greek peristyle house, and the Etruscan atrium house, all of which combined to become the Roman atrium house, a home designed around one or several internal gardens. The atrium was a patio with a skylight opening and a central pool for collecting rainwater. A larger patio, the peristyle, was surrounded by a covered colonnade, creating a shaded periphery around the garden. The patio, paved with a mosaic floor, brought the landscape, fountains, statues, light, and fresh air into the interior rooms. It had the extra benefit of privacy and security. The entire Mediterranean basin was the home of the Greek and Roman empires, whose architecture was mimicked by succeeding generations, including those in Spain.

This patio house had an unpretentious, windowless facade on the narrow street in contrast to the sumptuous fresco-painted walls on the interior. Since the Roman Empire encompassed the Mediterranean, its architectural traditions became the architectural traditions of that region. The concept of a court house fitted perfectly the personality of the Mediterranean—bright sun and strong light. The North African Moors' court house had two interior patios—the *dar* (a court without a garden) and the *riad* (with an interior garden). The Moors reintroduced the court house to the Iberian Peninsula and started the evolution of the Spanish patio house in Catalonia and Andalusia.

The Spanish court house fit perfectly into the climate of the Spanish colonies such as Cuba, both during and after colonial rule. Here family life centered on the landscaped patio to which all principal rooms opened. The Spanish patio brought a human scale to the home, a function of relativity, because in its enclosed space the scale was related to the small details of the home and garden. Without the enclosure of a high wall or patio, the garden home, nude to the street, would lose its human scale when compared to the relatively large expanses of the exterior communal land of the street and neighborhood. Upon entering a residence from the dust and noise of the busy street, a Habanero found himself enchanted by a serene and contemplative environment of the Spanish colonial patio with its fountain and feeling of calm. Havana's patio houses had additional advantages: a relatively high density within the city, which encourages the attributes of a rich city life; security; a flexible orientation to maximize sunlight; the introduction of carefully shaded, reflected, and diffused natural light into the rooms; harmony with the streetscape created by the close proximity of the street facade; an open landscaped interior available to all

The early Spanish mansions had a massive, tall arcade surrounding the ground-floor court to accommodate the traditional mezzanine. The courtyard provided natural light, softened by shade, and natural ventilation that entered the residence and all its spaces. Havana's Spanish colonial architects were masters at controlling sunlight. Tropical direct sunlight is harsh, creating sharp shadows, glare, and unwanted heat. They used sunlight effectively in the interior spaces by scattering it through reflection, diffusion, and even distribution, allowing daylight to penetrate deep into the core of the home.

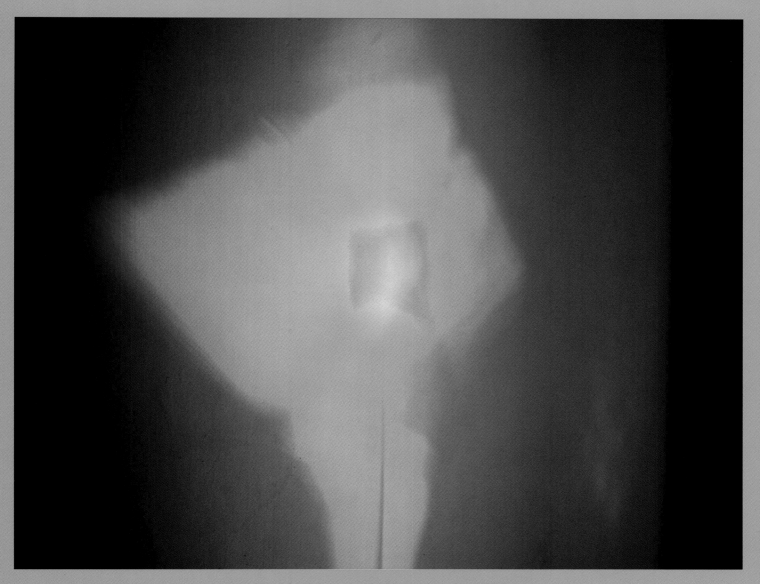

La Quinta de los Molinos—projected light cast from the *mediopunto* window. These typical Cuban stained-glass windows were used to frame the door or window openings and to diffuse the harsh tropical light while creating an ever-changing work of kinetic art, bringing splashes of colored sunlight that move throughout the home at different times of the day. They were originally created in the mid-eighteenth century and give Havana and the Cuban culture its unique sparkle.

Habana Vieja, the Real Fabrica de Tabaco Partagás, Calle Industria, No. 502. Built in 1845 as Cuba's largest cigar factory, it was located behind El Capitolio Nacional. It is famous for making Montecristo and Partagás cigars.

the principal living areas of the home; privacy; the elimination of street noises; the inclusion of a central or wall fountain to add the sound and refreshing movement of water that the Moors perfected so well; and good ventilation from the natural breezes created by the patio.

The Tobacco Factories

Cuba's prosperous tobacco industry, whose cigar manufacturing and export were centered in its capital, not only provided wealth and fame but also a rich history in graphic design, lithography, and art. In addition to Havana's residential mansions, Spanish colonial architecture's large central courts worked well for Havana's *tabaquerías* (tobacco factories). The ground floor was used for the storage of tobacco, where accessibility to the street was important. The central courtyard, covered with a glass roof, was perfectly suited for the dampening of the *majado* (tobacco leaves), for the initial manufacturing process, and for baling tobacco for export. The other operations—the selection of leaves, the removal of the leaf's stem, and administrative functions—took place on the *entresuelo* (mezzanine level). The top floor, with its maximum light, was perfect for rolling, wrapping, classifying, boxing, and storing of the finished cigars before shipment.

Tobacco, an indigenous product of the island, has always been an important part of the Cuban economy. It was originally brought to Spain in the sixteenth century for medicinal use. In the seventeenth century, tobacco became the New World's most desired luxury and Cuba's main export until it was replaced by sugar in the nineteenth century. European aristocracy, both men and women, fell in love with snuff as it became fashionable both in the Old World and the New World. By the end of the eighteenth century, Cuba was exporting 3,000 tons per year, and the tobacco industry, controlled by a few wealthy Spanish and Creole landowners, helped create a fine lifestyle and build many of the mansions of Havana.

Large tobacco factories, a relatively clean industry that needed an abundant source of manual labor, were perfect for the in-town locations of Havana. In the mid and late nineteenth century, large factories were built

The art of stone lithography, started in 1796, found its zenith in the printing of cigar label art, an integral part of the Cuban culture.

POR LARRAÑAGA

MADE IN HAVANA, CUBA

MARCA INDEPENDIENTE DE TABACOS DE VUELTA ABAJO.

LARRAÑAGA

in the new neighborhoods created outside the original walls, employing thousands of Habaneros. Real Fábrica de Tabaco Partagás, the largest in the city, was built in 1845 near El Capitolio. La Corona factory (1888) was built near Paseo del Prado. Cigar workers paid a lector (reader) to sit in a pulpit overlooking the work area and read newspapers, novels, or ballads.[3] The owners built magnificent mansions near these factories, a unique urban phenomenon. However, the inevitable clash between these areas and the working-class neighborhoods created for the workers produced an incentive for wealthy Habaneros to flee to the new suburban neighborhoods for refuge as Havana expanded.[4] Vincent Ybor, when the Ten Years' War started in 1868, moved his Havana cigar factory to Key West, Florida, and, when it later burned, transferred to Tampa, which became the neighborhood of Ybor City.

Case de la Obra Pia

The Casa de la Obra Pía (House of Charitable Works) (1665) is a gem of Spanish colonial architecture located on Calle Obra Pía (Pious Act Street) in Habana Vieja. It was beautifully restored in 1983. The house was so named because of the charity performed by Don Martín Calvo de la Puerta y Arrieta, who occupied the home in 1669. As a Spanish nobleman of wealth and philanthropy, he gave an annual dowry to five orphaned young girls to help them either to get married or to enter a convent.

The house later became the residence of Don Agustin de Cárdenas, who was named a marquis in honor of his part in the defense of Havana during the British siege in 1762. In 1703 the home was enlarged and refined and is today one of Havana's most beautiful Cuban baroque mansions. This house once reverberated with the happy sounds of young noblewomen enjoying their lavish coming-out balls when they were presented to Havana's society.

The home's architectural proportions and scale seem perfect for the gentle but aristocratic life of Habana Vieja. The home is stately yet informal, presenting a well-balanced composition as it wraps around its lushly landscaped central patio, where light and air bathe the family. The shaded, second-level gallery has a series of well-proportioned columns and arches that give a lyrical, almost musical rhythm to the patio. The color palette of the restored home is a beautiful yellow trimmed with white integrate moldings and capitals. The entire color scheme is accented with a rich blue on the balustrade, stair banister, French doors, and window grills. Along the base of the gallery, a series of horizontal bands of patterned ceramic tile act as a base and a wainscot.

The family's second-floor peripheral rooms open through a wide, arched entryway to this gallery and the patio beyond. In this way those in each room enjoy the light breeze, aroma, and view of the vine-covered garden.

Casa de la Obra Pía. Both photographs illustrate the joining of the interior and exterior spaces: one with open doors and one with filtered light piercing through the *mediopunto* side-lights and *persiana* doors.

The interiors are light and airy with an exposed beam ceiling now painted blue, and a marble floor that acts as a base for the richly carved mahogany furniture. Suspended pennants with iron-and-glass-sculptured fixtures provide the lighting. Sculptures on pedestals at strategic locations draw the eye to increase the drama of each perspective when experiencing the house.

The Spanish colonial homes were introverted, with family privacy and intimacy of prime concern. This represented the self-contained world of a home as a retreat from the often hectic world of the city. However, as Havana grew, it started to consider landscaped public spaces as essential to the well-being of the city. It then started to copy the model of the emerging American suburbs and its garden city concept, where the public view of the residence, with its landscape and particularly its taste and wealth, became of paramount consideration.

Casa de la Obra Pía. An arched gallery, the shaded intermediate space seamlessly joins the interiors to the lushly landscaped central courtyard.

El Capitolio Nacional (now the offices and library of the Cuban Academy of Sciences) (1929).
Architects: Raúl Otero, Evelio Govantes, Félix Cabarrocas, José M. Bens Arrarte, Eugenio
Rayneri Piedra, and others.

Chapter 6

A String of Public Spaces

Parque Central. Stately native royal palms create a strong vertical element between
Manzana de Gómez on the left and the Palacio del Centro Asturiano on the right.

HAVANA'S PUBLIC PLACES are just like outdoor rooms, enclosed by a parade of surrounding eclectic facades that quietly whisper, "I am part of the neighborhood, part of the city." These outdoor rooms are bounded by the sky and tree canopy above, defined on their sides by buildings and gardens, with a floor of stone pavement or grass. These outdoor rooms of Havana offer the Habaneros spaces with a variety of style, texture, color, and landscape. Havana's public gardens create an interlocking sequence of human experiences that give the Habaneros a sense of position and identity within the city, a feeling of personal connection to the city.[1]

Any city, in order to call itself a great city, must have an abundance of public green spaces for its citizenry to rest, relax, meet friends, nap, and play, or perhaps just enjoy a small touch of nature. Havana does not have one grand park like New York's Central Park (Frederick Law Olmsted and Calvert Vaux, 1857–1873), or Barcelona's Parc Güell (Antonio Gaudí, 1900–1914) or its Parc de la Ciutabella (Josep Fontseré and Antonio Gaudí, 1888), but it does have a continuous series of green public spaces, a ring of green, much like central London's chain of parks (St. James's Park, Green Park, Buckingham Palace Gardens, Hyde Park, Regent's Park, and Kensington Gardens) or Daniel Burnham's creation of Chicago's Lake Shore Drive on Lake Michigan (1894–1909), which was a complex network of parkways of curves, views, public gardens, and squares.

Havana's green promenade system is an urban string of emeralds, a ring of public spaces that is one of the most beautiful in the Americas. It starts with Parque de la Fraternidad (Brotherhood Park, 1892), then flows into the Jardínes del Capitolio, the large landscaped area in front of El Capitolio (the National Capitol). It then passes the Palacio del Centro Gallego to Parque Central (Central Park), the stately town square, which flows into the linear promenaded park Paseo del Prado, which in turn leads into the Malecón, skirting the Caribbean Sea. This series of continuous, open, picturesque public parks weaves its way through Central Habana. This marriage between city and trees started developing in 1863 when the original city walls were demolished to make room for the expanding city.

Parque de la Fraternidad

Parque de la Fraternidad was created in 1892 to celebrate the 400-year anniversary of Columbus's arrival to the New World. The park has La fuente de la India (fountain of the Indian girl), or La fuente de Noble Habana (fountain of Noble Habana),

Parque de la Fraternidad, with the Árbol de la Fraternidad Americana and the Cuban Telephone
Company Building beyond. The park was built in 1892 on old Campo de Marte (the military
drill square) to commemorate the fourth centennial of Columbus's discovery of America.

Parque de la Fraternidad, with the Árbol de la Fraternidad Americana.

Parque de la Fraternidad. The bottom photo is looking toward the Fuente de la India Noble Habana.

which faces El Capitolio from Parque de la Fraternidad. This fountain has a white marble sculpture of a crowned Grecian maiden, an allegorical symbolic of Havana, sitting on a throne above four dolphins spouting water into the fountain below. This sculpture and fountain—still held in affection by the Habaneros—was presented to the city by the Count of Villanueva, who had originally owned this land as his country estate. Parque de la Fraternidad was originally part of a larger square, Campo de Marte (Field of Mars), located at the end of Paseo del Prado. In the nineteenth century, Campo de Marte was used by the Spanish military to hold their drills. Illuminated by gas lamps, the square was a place for leisure in the heart of the city. During carnival time, it was the starting point for the city's carnival parades. It was originally called Colon Park, which, in itself, comprised another park—the diminutive La India Park.

On February 24, 1928, Colon Park was redesigned to become Fraternity Park, on the occasion of the Sexta Conference International Americana (the Sixth Pan-American Conference), which was held in Havana. It was rededicated to show the solidarity of Cuba with the other countries of the Americas. Joining President Calvin Coolidge in Havana for this conference were twenty-one heads of state of the Americas.

The solidarity and the fraternal affection of the Americas with Havana were symbolized by the planting of the Tree of the Fraternidad Americana in soil generated from samples provided by each of the participating countries. The Tree of the Fraternidad Americana is a cottonwood tree that the important art and social magazine *Social* called the "poor ceiba." (The ceiba tree was a symbolic tree, sacred to American Indians such as the Maya, who planted them in symmetrical, landscaped plazas.) The tree was surrounded by a beautiful raised circular bronze rail with the coats of arms of the countries of the Americas. The Tree of the Fraternidad Americana, now spreading and mature, is one of the rare occurrences where a tree has become a living and important monument within a city.

Jardínes del Capitolio

The next public urban garden on this ring of parks is the Jardínes del Capitolio (the National Capitol's Gardens), located just southwest of Parque Central.[2] These gardens and their neighbor, the Parque de la Fraternidad, were part of the overall planning for Cuba's new capitol building, El Capitolio Nacional.

In front and on the sides of El Capitolio Nacional, this imposing neoclassical edifice to the new republic, Jean Claude Nicolas Forestier planned a grand public square, creating a smooth transition between the new Parque de la Fraternidad and the Palacio del Centro Gallego (now the Gran Teatro de la Habana, 1915) adjoin-

El Capitolio Nacional with Jean Claude Nicolas Forestier's designed landscape—with the monument Fuente de la India Noble Habana in the foreground as seen from the Parque de la Fraternidad.

ing Parque Central. Capitolio Square is articulated by a series of handsome white marble and iron streetlights set amid a pattern of low plantings surrounding tall royal palms (which Forestier loved as native to Cuba) aligned against and complementing the classical, colonnaded building. The architectural design of El Capitolio has two hemicycles at either end: one for the Chamber of Deputies and the other for the Parliament, both set in symmetrical gardens. These gardens were to have had two large baroque fountains to cap this dynamic presence, but they were never executed.

El Capitolio Nacional

El Capitolio Nacional, constructed and inaugurated by President Gerardo Machado on May 20, 1929, the twenty-seventh anniversary of the Republic of Cuba, is one of the most striking capitol buildings in the world. Built on the site of Havana's first railroad station at a cost of $17 million, it was the seat of Cuba's House of Representatives and the Senate until the Communist revolution and is similar in appearance to the U.S. Capitol in Washington, D.C.

A grand granite staircase leads into El Capitolio, with its imposing facade of classical columns. The exterior was constructed of Cuban limestone, while the interior was lavishly embellished with marble, mahogany, and bronze. Behind the staircase and the perron (the exterior platform leading into the building) are four bronze doors with bas-reliefs portraying important events of Cuban history. At the head of the grand stairs are two flanking bronze heroic statues by sculptor Angelo Zanelli that symbolize "work" and "virtue," the artist's concept as the tutelaries of the town.

El Capitolio's dome was the highest point in Havana (300 feet) until the 1950s and is visible from almost any point in the city. Inside and directly below this dome was the Statue of the Republic, a twenty-two-karat gold leaf, bronze statue, fifty-six feet tall and weighing forty-nine tons, sculpted by Zanelli. In front of the statue, embedded in the marble floor in the building's center, was a twenty-four-karat diamond with thirty-two facets, marking the point from which all Cuban roads are measured. The diamond, from Kimberley, South Africa, originally belonged to the Russian tsar but was replaced by a copy in 1973.

El Capitolio runs parallel to the original Hotel Pasaje, which harmoniously defines another urban plaza. Architecture is often compared to frozen music, and the juxtaposition of this building with El Capitolio reminds one of a professional ballroom dance couple: El Capitolio being the beautiful, swirling woman and the straight Hotel Pasaje building her tall, elegant partner.

El Capitolio Nacional, a monumental building that was the symbol of the new republic, is graciously silhouetted against the clear Cuban sky. Its construction started in 1925 and finished in 1929, with an area of 480,000 square feet on two city blocks. Up to 6,000 men worked day and night in eight-hour shifts. The cost, including furniture, was over $16 million.

Salón de los Pasos Perdidos—official reception hall of El Capitolio Nacional, in the Renaissance style, 400 feet long and 45 feet wide. The massive bronze doors at each end of the hall, designed by Enrique Garcia Cabrera, weigh 2.5 tons each. There are thirty-two bronze candelabras plus indirect lighting in the cornice. The ceiling is delicately hand-painted with twenty-two-karat gold leaf.

Above: Salons of state.

Left: The Capitol Dome, located in the center of the Reception Hall, has a total height from the street level of 308 feet, the third highest dome in the world. It was designed with a *centellador* (beacon of light) on the top, which can be seen throughout Havana.

Above: Jardínes del Capitolio (Capitol Gardens), with Palacio del Centro Gallego behind. Here Jean Claude Nicolas Forestier fashioned a formal landscaped setting in keeping with the majesty of the capitol of the new republic. Modular pavers, granite and iron light standards, and native plantings extended the neoclassic capitol's architecture into the public domain. A monument and symbol is not treated as a work of "celebrity architecture" but as a seamless marriage of architecture, culture, and the city.

Preceding pages: Coffering squares of polygonal ornamentation in the ceiling of the Chamber of Deputies.

Hotel Pasaje

The Hotel Pasaje (Passageway Hotel), built in 1876, was Havana's first modern hotel. This hotel had an amazing new invention—an elevator. The hotel had a large iron and glass arcade traversing its ground level, with shops lining either side that pierced the building through two tall arched entrances on either end. The hotel collapsed in a storm, although its facade was restored and preserved while the inside of the hotel was replaced by a boxing arena.

Anchoring the end of this long building and bordering the Parque Central was the Teatro Payret, a theater that opened in 1877. It was renamed the Teatro de la Paz (Theater of Peace) in honor of the Treaty of Zanjón in 1878. Owned by Catalonian Joaquín Payret, it could entertain 2,000 patrons at one sitting. It was converted into Cuba's first motion picture house in 1897 and in 1940 was modernized to become Havana's premier movie house.

Parque Central

Next on this ring is Parque Central, what Forestier called the "Republican Forum," where again the stately royal palms become the columns echoing the surrounding colonnaded facades. The park, also known as Parque José Martí, dates back to 1903 and is enclosed by beautifully ornamented early-nineteenth-century rococo, baroque, and Spanish Renaissance buildings and open-air cafés.

Parque Central is the pulsing heart of Havana, a large rectangular park paved and landscaped with flowering tropical plants that flourish in the sun while walkers enjoy the shade of the royal palms, laurels, and royal poinciana trees. Habaneros pass through this square ceaselessly, so that it is never completely deserted, night or day. Habaneros organized groups of friends who regularly met in the park to gossip and discuss politics and their everyday lives. The park was flanked by open-air cafés, where the orchestras rivaled each other for the quality of their rumba music.

Hotel Pasaje (Passageway Hotel) (1876)—Havana's first modern hotel. El Capitolio Nacional (1929) is directly across from this building, defining another wonderful public square (1876).

Parque Central. A well-defined urban park focuses on the statue of José Martí, Cuba's national hero, which in turn is set against the background of the Hotel Inglaterra (1836), a historic hotel. This park links the Jardínes del Capitolio and the Prado Promenade, continuing the string of public places that unite the inner city.

Parque Central. Royal palms, the stately "architecturally correct" native Cuban tree, frame the statue of José Martí.

Palacio del Centro Gallego, now the Gran Teatro de la Habana, seen from the Jardínes del Capitolio. Architect: Paul Belau, 1915. Sculptor: Guiseppe Moretti.

Palacio del Centro Gallego.

After independence was accomplished, José Martí's Carrara marble statue replaced the original statue of Queen Isabella II in the middle of the park. Known as the "Apostol" of Cuban liberty (1905), his statue points significantly to Obispo Street, where shops and commerce flourish. According to the monument's sculptor, José Vilalta de Saavedra, Martí is addressing the Cuban people after giving them the single-starred banner of freedom furled at Zanjón, which inspired Cubans to begin the War of Independence (1895–1898). On the pedestal in high relief are nineteen figures, all eagerly straining toward the goal of independence. Overshadowing this assemblage is a Winged Victory bearing aloft the palm of peace.

Palacio del Centro Gallego

In the nineteenth century, it became fashionable for Habaneros born in Spain to build monumental cultural and social clubs for each regional immigrant group. The most imposing of these and the park's neighbor (defining both the Jardines del Capitolio and Parque Central) is the Palacio del Centro Gallego, now the Gran Teatro de la Habana (the National Theatre). It was built in 1915 on the original site of the Teatro Nuevo, also called the Teatro Tacón (built in 1837), which was, in its day, the most prestigious theater in Havana.

The Palacio del Centro Gallego was an architecturally sumptuous social club and theater for the large group of Spaniards who emigrated from Galicia, Spain, to Havana. Its rich embellishments envelop the building, casting myriad shadows into its deep recesses as the Cuban sunlight sparkles on its projecting elements. The verticality of its pilasters are capped by arches and punctuated by graceful, sculptural round balconies. The pedestal for this palace is the typical solid recessed arcade, while its crowning glory is a symphony of pinnacles and soaring cupolas high on the corner towers, capped by winged bronze maidens sharply silhouetted against the blue sky. It was the most expensive building built in Cuba in its day.

The Palacio del Centro Gallego's ballroom held galas where 2,000 society couples could feast and dance. It housed one of the world's largest opera houses, inaugurated with Verdi's *Aida*, and the greatest singers and actors of the day performed in this theater. This grand theater and concert hall is now the home of the superb Ballet Nacional de Cuba, one of the finest ballet companies in the world.

Palacio del Centro Asturiano

Another important neighbor of the park is the Palacio del Centro Asturiano (1927), a mutual benefit and cultural society with a membership of about 70,000. Inside its classical Spanish Renaissance, four-story, arcaded exterior is an amazing theatrical interior with a grand gallery containing a marble monumental staircase, a famous tiled bar, and a stained-glass ceiling portraying the arrival of Columbus. Its facade

Palacio del Centro Asturiano (1927) from Parque Central.

Parque Central—Hotel Inglaterra, with the statue of José Marti in the foreground.

Left: Lobby, Hotel Inglaterra, Art Nouveau bronze statue of a flamenco dancer with Andalusian tile mosaic behind.

Below: The inspiration for the Hotel Inglaterra, and for much of the architectural flavor of Havana, can be found in Spanish and Andalusian culture, such as the flamenco dancers shown here.

is a layering of four horizontal bands articulated by its rhythmical black arcade and windows. However, its crowning glory, silhouetted against the sky, are three circular towers on three of its corners and an amazingly beautiful octagonal tower on the fourth side facing the park. These sumptuous, regional social centers as works of architecture became competitive in design and construction with Havana's grand government buildings of the state and the palaces of its aristocracy.[3]

Hotel Inglaterra

Also edging and central to the Parque Central is the baroque Hotel Inglaterra (Hotel England), sometimes called the Inglaterra Grand Hotel and Restaurant, the city's oldest and one of its most elegant hotels, dating from 1875. The hotel added a well-blended addition on the adjoining property in 1890. It was constructed on the original location of the well-known Acera del Louvre, where students would gather to talk against Spanish rule. Its central location, symmetrically facing Parque Central and, since 1905, behind the park's José Martí statue and adjoining the Palacio del Centro Gallego, has added to its fame, attracting through the years celebrities as prominent as Sarah Bernhardt.

The hotel's facade is dignified and simple, with a colonnaded base of deep shadows, then three floors of balconies and applied embellishments, crowned by a decorative parapet and distinctive Hotel Inglaterra sign in its center. The hotel's most famous symbol is the Art Nouveau bronze statue of a flamenco dancer, surrounded by Moorish geometric tiles imported from Seville, which greets guests at the bar and sets the hotel's Andalusia, Mudejar (Moorish) theme.

Plaza Hotel

The Plaza Hotel, a fine nineteenth-century colonnaded hotel, touches at a sharp but handsome angle the corner of the Parque Central. It was originally a private palace and then the home of *El Diario de la Marina*, an influential newspaper. Converted into one of Havana's finest hotels in 1901 by an American who was part of the American occupying government, Captain W. Fletcher Smith, it opened for business in 1909 and had a clean, sharp fenestration crowned by a wonderful pergola-topped roof garden and terrace added in 1919, along with a new ballroom. From 1985 to 1991 the hotel underwent a major renovation/restoration.

Its architectural proportions, as well as its guest list, are similar to its neighbor, the Hotel Inglaterra. Its guests included celebrities such as Isadora Duncan, Enrico Caruso, and Anna Pavlova.

The importance of the corner in urban planning is illustrated by the Plaza Hotel. Its general mass, with its Cuban flag flying high, is a simple arrow that points right at the Parque Central, its most important neighbor. The hotel's arcaded shape is like an unfolding fan that seems to greet all. It is easy to see and feel the graciousness of the entrance, its central focal point. The corner of the hotel is clipped, creating a minisquare at its front. The cutting of a building's corners at intersections in Central Habana was a wonderful concept adapted by Havana's codes from an idea conceived by Catalonian planner Ildefons Cerdà at a time when Barcelona's walls came down and the city expanded (see chapter 10).

The Plaza Hotel, a fine nineteenth-century colonnaded hotel, corner of Parque Central.

Paseo del Prado—a pedestrian mall.

Chapter 7

Paseo del Prado

Main Street of the City

Hotel Sevilla Biltmore, Habana, Cuba.

THE PRADO, the most wonderful and historic *paseo* in Havana, is the city's main street. It is part of the ring of parks (discussed in chapter 6) that start at Castillo de San Salvador de la Punta and the Malecón, then run up the Prado, past the Parque Central and the Jardínes del Capitolio, and end at the Parque de la Fraternidad. The Prado, officially called Paseo de Martí, was originally a grand neighborhood of the very rich west and south of the city's walls that fell into decay as the occupants gradually moved elsewhere. But after full renovation by the French city planner and landscape architect Jean Claude Nicolas Forestier in 1929, the Prado regained, and perhaps even superseded, its former glory. It has been affectionately called the Champs-Élysées of Havana.

From an urban design perspective, it is a long residential garden street, a linear public park that provides in its central wide pavement a place for children to play and for neighbors to meet, rest, or even sleep on one of the many park benches under the shade of the spreading canopy of trees. The Prado's construction and history are both longer than its half-mile length might imply.

As discussed in Part I, the Marqués de la Torre created the Prado, then known as Alameda de Isabella II, between 1772 and 1852 for the city's aristocrats to parade up and down its full length riding high in their *volantas* to greet and see their friends. It was a place just outside the city walls where one could breathe the fresh air not easily found in the dense confines of the walled city. In those days, five bands were placed along the drive to entertain the members of high society as they rode past. As is often the case in the evolution of a city, other locales eventually caught the eye of the Alameda de Isabella II residents, and the area lost its appeal as the prime area for Havana's high society. As a result, the *volantas* dispersed. and the area fell into disrepair.

During the American military government rule in Cuba under General Leonard Wood at the turn of the twentieth century, concrete paving was laid the full length of its central walk. With this new surface, it then became a wonderful place for carnivals and military parades. Then, in 1937, Jean Claude Nicolas Forestier made Paseo del Prado a salon within the city, setting its sophisticated and tranquil mood.[1] In Forestier's city plan, it became a visual link between the new Capitolio, on the western corner of Parque Central, and Malecón and Castillo de San Salvador de la Punta and the sea.

Sevilla Biltmore Hotel on the Paseo del Prado (1908, with a ten-story addition in 1917) whose lobby spaces were built in a neo-Moorish style.

Forestier elevated the linear, central pedestrian walk and paved it with multicolored, geometric patterns. The walls of this outdoor room were the flanking trees and coral rock benches that defined the space. Eight bronze lions, symbolizing the strength of Havana, were added to complement the elegant, wrought-iron, baroque streetlamps that were set on raised, coral-rock pedestals.

Facing Paseo del Prado are beautiful and stately porticoed mansions with Old World refinement. These were built in the late nineteenth and early twentieth centuries by the rising entrepreneurial class. At the time, Paseo del Prado became the most desirable residential avenue on which to live. The street's collection of eclectic architecture includes the Centro de Dependientes del Comercio (Center for Shop Clerks, 1902–1907), a three-story, neoclassical, colonnaded building designed by Arturo Amigó, a wonderful example of the recreational social clubs built in Havana at the turn of the twentieth century as a testament to the commercial prosperity of the city. Then there is the Teatro Fausto (1938), built on the same site as the original theater of the same name, and the historic Hotel Sevilla, which opened on Paseo del Prado in 1908, with its rusticated facade. When it opened, it was Havana's premier hotel, with the luxury of private bathrooms, electric lights, and telephones. Its ten-story tower was added in 1917, with its scale dominating Paseo del Prado. In 1924 its name was changed to the Sevilla Biltmore Hotel.

Paseo del Prado, with its homes, office buildings, theaters, and cafés, was a giant outdoor garden room well defined on its flanks, with a ribbon of pavement shaded by an overhanging laurel canopy and the blue sky peeking through the tracery of branches. Paseo del Prado is a multitiered system of pedestrian and vehicular lanes: first, on its outside border, are the covered colonnaded arcades and sidewalks that hug and are an integral part of the parade of stately buildings; then the motorway; next, the raised border of trees, rows of benches, and streetlights; then, finally, the central paved recreation and pedestrian walk occasionally peppered with public fountains. This entire diverse use of urban layering is then repeated symmetrically on the other side, making Paseo del Prado the grand boulevard that it is.

Preceding pages: Paseo del Prado—"The urban living room of Havana."

Opposite, top: Centro de Dependientes del Comercio, Calle Morro y Paseo del Prado (1902–1907).

Opposite, bottom: Paseo del Prado—the Teatro Fausto (1938), by Cuban architect Saturnino Parajón. This Art Deco building was a popular movie theater that specialized in foreign films in the 1950s, a favorite of one of the authors who courted his sweetheart (who then became his wife) there while accompanied by a chaperone.

Fuente de la India Noble Habana (1837).

Paseo del Prado—General historic view of the Alameda de Isabella II and the Fuente de la India Noble Habana. Originally, the *paseo* was named after Queen Isabella of Spain, but later it was called the Paseo de Martí and more commonly Paseo del Prado.

Paseo del Prado—neo-Moorish residence (ca. 1910), typical of the early-twentieth-century eclectic architecture that enlivens the neighborhoods of Havana.

Havana is a city of small squares with large doses of Cuban history. Pictured here is a statue (1938) honoring Cuban poet Juan Clemente Zenea (1834–1871). Zenea founded the *Revista Habanera* in 1861, and when the Cuban insurrection began in 1868, he published a newspaper in New York supporting the Cuban patriots. In 1870 he was sent to Cuba by the revolutionary committee and was imprisoned in La Cabaña Fort, court-martialed, and shot. Zenea enjoys a wide reputation as a lyrical poet in Spanish-speaking countries.

Part III

The City's Neighborhoods in the First Half of the Twentieth Century

Chapter 8

The Malecón

La Fachada of Havana

El Malecón de Havana (Avenida del Golfo, 1902). The powerful sea meets the land, blurring the line between humans and nature.

AVENIDA ANTONIO MACEO, known as the Paseo del Malecón, or the Malecón, is the waterfront promenade and drive that was started in 1901 and was built on reclaimed land bordering the Gulf of Mexico. Lining and defining the Malecón is a continuous row of low residential buildings whose colonnaded arcades mirror the architectural theme established within the city. This pedestrian and automobile promenade connects Paseo del Prado with the sea. As it developed, it connected old and Central Havana with its new district of Miramar and Country Club Park.

The first proposal for a boulevard along the Havana waterfront was made by Cuban engineer Francisco de Albear in 1874 when he completed the Plano de Havana as part of his project for supplying water to the city. The proposal was never realized, but it was an important precedent for the American engineers during the administration of General Leonard Wood. American engineer W. J. Barden finally designed the boulevard, which had on both its flanks a wide sidewalk. One sidewalk was constructed in front of the required arcades for the new buildings, the other in front of the seawall bordering the ocean. Decorative cast-iron lights illuminated the entire boulevard.

Initial Phase of the American Design of the Malecón

The American administration was able to build eleven blocks of the Malecón from Paseo del Prado to Lealtad Street. This seaside boulevard was originally called Avenida del Golfo, later Avenida de la Republica, and, in 1908, Avenida Antonio Maceo. The original Malecón had two areas with unique character. The first were the six blocks from Paseo del Prado to Galiano Street. Here the street pattern was irregular. Streets in this area were the oldest outside the walls. This irregular design then changes in orientation at San Lazaro, and more regular streets occur, creating one-block inland views from the Malecón.

The special pastime for the Habaneros at the turn of the twentieth century was to promenade down Paseo del Prado to the sea and on to where the Malecón begins, and then stroll from the Castillo de San Salvador de la Punta to the San Lazaro cove. At the *castillo*, at the point where the land juts out toward the bay's channel and where the boats parade by, there was a small classic *glorieta* (bandstand), destroyed in 1926, where popular open-air concerts were held.

The street pattern changes in the second area, located west of Galiano. Here there are long straight streets allowing for extended views from the waterfront around the city. Small buildings dominate the architecture of this area. Two- and three-story buildings with narrow frontage on the Malecón create the environment of a small city, despite the fact that this area, when it was being built, was just a short walk from the center of the city.

Antonio Maceo Park

The next segment of the Malecón one comes to is totally different. Completed in 1916, it contains the largest area of land reclaimed from the sea. It has an esplanade and small urban park, Antonio Maceo Park, designed by Domenico Boni, a well-known Italian sculptor. Antonio Maceo Park creates an open plaza in front of the ocean and gives another pedestrian edge to the city. It is one of the most successful urban designs on Havana's waterfront.

Plaza del Maine

After a short transition of six blocks, the waterfront changes again. The Malecón becomes the edge of a large esplanade and small urban park for the monument to the victims of the sinking of the U.S. battleship *Maine*, the Monumento a las Víctimas del Maine. This is Cuba's handsome memorial in honor of the heroes—two officers and 258 crewmen—of the USS *Maine*, mysteriously blown up on February 15, 1898, in Havana Harbor. Two months later the United States declared war against Spain, starting the Spanish-American War, largely because of public resentment and excitement whipped up by the battle cry "Remember the Maine!" Iron cannons and chains salvaged from the decks of the ill-fated battleship were used to build this memorial.

The edges of this important central area of the city are defined by Paseo del Prado, which was part of the Reparto de las Murallas; the Malecón, the "urban balcony" of the city in front of the Atlantic Ocean and to the west; and Avenida de los Presidentes, one of the most beautiful streets of the Reparto del Vedado. In this section of the Malecón there is a symbolic walkway from the Capitolio Nacional complex to the oceanfront, beginning at the Malecón and continuing all the way to Avenida de los Presidentes in El Vedado and ending at the Monumento a José Miguel Gómez near La Quinta de los Molinos, the summer residence of the Spanish military governors (see chapter 11). Inside this urban amphitheater, selected sites and monuments act as focal points and share with other parts of Havana the urban traditions, problems and, hopefully, opportunities to serve as a foundation for future changes to the city.

REPUBLICA DE CUBA
SECRETARIA DE OBRAS PUBLICAS
PLAZA DEL MAINE.   JULIO.16.1930   NO 11.186

Plaza del Maine, El Malecón y Avenida. A wonderful example of gracious beaux-arts design superimposed on and enriching the street pattern of the seaside boulevard, the Malecón. The plaza focuses on the handsome memorial built in 1926 in honor of those who died on the USS *Maine*. In the following photo, one should notice that the eagle at the top of the monument was removed by Castro as an anti-American action.

The Monument to General Máximo Gómez

The Monument to General Máximo Gómez (1935) pays tribute to this Dominican, who was called El Generalisimo and who commanded Cuba's liberation army during the Cuban War of Independence. Sculpted by Aldo Gamba, it consists of exquisitely carved white marble figures, highlighted by two bronze sculptures—one of the general on his triumphant stallion high on top of a classical temple, and the other an expressive sculpture of fierce, intertwined horses and beautiful women emerging with a powerful force of bronze and gushing water from the sculpture's pedestal cascading into a fountain below. Two important avenues define one side of the plaza: Calle 23 and Calle Infanta.

In addition to the intermittent parks and monuments that visually relieve the lineal spatial form and vistas along the Malecón, a gracious park sits in front of the legendary Hotel Nacional, giving its visitors and guests a wonderful view of the sea. This park and its gradual ascent to the hotel provide a sweeping green lawn that is unencumbered by objects except for a solitary black historic cannon.

The architectural firm McKim, Mead, and White designed the Hotel Nacional (1930) in Vedado, one the best-known hotels in Havana, and still the finest. The hotel is located across from the Monumento a las Víctimas del Maine on top of a promontory that was used as a base for Spanish artillery.

The rest of the Malecón, up to Avenida de los Presidentes, was completed in 1926 and is now dominated by tall apartment buildings that lack the quality, scale, and thoughtfulness of structures built in the older areas of the Malecón.

While most of Havana is an urban landscape, the Malecón joins the fortresses of the city as a powerful seascape. In a one-and-a-half-mile walk along the Malecón, the feeling of nature, history, and architecture is a unique experience. One will discover changes from block to block, an unfolding historical, architectural journey with a pleasant urban continuity. The Habaneros love the Malecón, for it is a park, a window to the sea, and a meeting place—all in one. It is an expression of the city's character: open, active, brave, or calm—depending on the season—but always an independent momentary respite from the constant collage of politics and world events. At the present time, the beautiful landmarks of Havana have disintegrated due to lack of maintenance.

Havana's monuments, such as the Monumento de Estudiantes de Medicina (the Medical Students' Monument) at the end of the Prado commemorating the unjust execution of eight medical students in 1871 by Spanish volunteers, are symbols of the city's history—urban punctuation marks—that are distant visual images that extend the view so that eyes can come to rest on a distant object of granite or bronze and complete the urban landscape.

El Malecón—monument to the victims of the USS *Maine* (1902).

Details of the Monumento al General Máximo Gómez. Gómez was the supreme commander of the revolutionary army in 1895. The statue was sculpted by the Italian artist Aldo Gamba in 1935. The site is now the entrance to the tunnel under the bay. This is in front of the Presidential Palace and near Castillo de la Punta.

Antonio Maceo Park and statue, Malecón. Belascoaín, San Lázaro, and Marina, Central Habana. Sculptor: Domenico Boni (1916).

Chapter 9

A New Urban Scale and Architectural Vocabulary

Hotel Nacional, Vedado—built on the hill that housed the Santa Clara gun battery and designed by McKim, Mead, and White. The main entrance drive (above) and the gracious, Spanish colonial loggia open to its central court (below). The soft wicker chairs invoke images of Caribbean comfort and tropical graciousness (1930).

THE WALLS OF Havana were torn down starting on August 8, 1863, and in 1865 the land occupied by those walls and beyond was for sale. The city then expanded in a continuous fashion throughout the first half of the twentieth century. This normal organic growth stopped when the city was put into suspended animation in 1959 by the Communist revolution.

The *repartos* (planned neighborhoods) El Carmelo, El Vedado, and Miramar were subdivisions that today dominate the urban form of Havana. One cannot discuss the physical dimensions of Havana without understanding and exploring El Carmelo, El Vedado, and Miramar. Often visitors and even historians concentrate on Habana Vieja or even Central Habana and ignore these important neighborhoods. They are important not only because they occupy a large section of the physical city but also because they were attempts on a grand scale to develop residential neighborhoods that would enhance, in a gracious and harmonious way, the quality of life of those who lived there. They were, to a great degree, prime real estate and therefore became the residential areas for the wealthiest within the expanding city.

El Carmelo and El Vedado

El Carmelo was a farm located between the Almendares River and another farm, El Vedado. Don José Domingo Trigo and Don Juan Espino, the owners of El Carmelo, hired engineer Luis Iboléon Bosque to design a subdivision on their farm, El Vedado. The city of Havana approved the development on April 8, 1859, nine years before the beginning of the Ten Years' War. The following year Don Francisco de Frías, Conde de Pozos Dulces, and his family also hired the same engineer to develop their farm, located between El Carmelo and the Battery of Santa Clara on the coast. El Carmelo merged with El Vedado, becoming the largest addition to the original settlement of Havana since its founding in 1519.

El Vedado encompassed an area containing 134 city blocks. It dedicated two blocks for future churches, three for markets, and one for a park. It was designed with streets 48 feet wide and blocks 305 by 305 feet square. Its design was to follow the American suburban prototype of low-density homes with exposed peripheral gardens as part of the shared landscape, as opposed to the higher-density traditional Spanish homes that focus internally on a central patio. Ordinances required minimums for a front garden of 15 feet and a porch 12 feet deep. El Vedado was designed to achieve a density of sixty-six residents per acre, considered a very low density for Havana at the end of nineteenth century.

The main urban features of El Vedado were, and still are, two principal avenues: Paseo and Avenida de los Presidentes, which is also called Avenue G; each is a spacious 150 feet wide. They both have a large, central, and beautifully landscaped parterre (a landscaped meridian), with roadways and garden-style homes flanking either side. Avenida de los Presidentes, the principal street of El Vedado, is a monumental path linking the waterfront to the hill of the Castillo del Princípe and an edge that divides the most dense and complex urban area with office buildings, hotels, and apartments from the still predominantly residential area. The inland end of the Avenida de los Presidentes is the monument of President José Miguel Gómez located in front of the Castillo del Príncipe and not far from La Quinta de los Molinos. One of the most beautiful monuments in the urban landscape of Havana, it is classic in its architecture style and is clearly visible, for it is perched high on a broad pedestal that adds a final punctuation point to the wonderful Avenida de los Presidentes. Beautifully executed, sweeping marble sculptures grace its roof and are clearly silhouetted against the clear blue Havana sky. The monument is oval in plan, and the visitors are enveloped by the architecture as they enter its defined central court.

Notwithstanding the wonderful boulevards and monuments, one limitation of the urban design of El Vedado is the poor articulation between its street pattern and the existing urbanized areas of the rest of Havana. This creates a very poorly organized connection between two of the city's most important real estate sites.

El Vedado and El Carmelo were not products of the "Garden Cities of Tomorrow," as championed by Ebenezer Howard in the late nineteenth century as self-contained cities of limited size and growth. Rather, they represented the American pattern of suburbia that merely widened the dormitory areas of the city.[1] This American suburban residential concept lined the houses in neat rows, as if on a neighborhood receiving line, presenting and displaying their architectural styles to the neighborhood and community.

Miramar: The Continuation of the Urbanization of the Oceanfront

Miramar was the beautiful *reparto* of Havana and the continuation of the urbanization of the city's oceanfront. El Vedado was growing rapidly at the beginning of the new republic as the Cuban economy recuperated from the War of Independence and the wealthy families were abandoning El Cerro as their favorite residential site. It was the most lucrative real estate of Havana, and soon developers started to plan ways to transfer the successful growth of El Vedado to other adjoining areas. The logical selection was the land across the Almendares River, the western boundary

Above and the following four pages: El Vedado—homes and apartments built during the first half of the twentieth century in the American style, often with porches or balconies opening to the street, and homes surrounded by small gardens.

Calle G ó Avenida de los Presidentes, Vedado—one of the most gracious and beautiful residential streets not only in Havana but in the world. Stately palms and generous landscaping separate the homes and seamlessly integrate the park with the neighborhood.

of the city of Havana. This new subdivision was initially called "El Nuevo Vedado" in sales promotions, but that name was abandoned around 1918 for Miramar.

Reparto Miramar was the result of the work of two people: Carlos Miguel de Céspedes and Luis Morales y Pedroso. A successful lawyer involved in land development and aware of urbanism theories and practices in Europe and the United States, Céspedes was secretary of public works from 1925 to 1929. He was a promoter of the construction of the Capitolio, the remodeling of Paseo del Prado, and the building of the national Carretera Central (the central highway linking all provincial capitals). He invited Jean Claude Nicolas Forestier, the world-renowned landscape planner, to plan the urban landscape of the city and to develop other projects in Cuba.

A descendant of the fourth Marqués de la Real Proclamación and an architect and engineer schooled in the United Status, Luis Morales y Pedroso was a cofounder, with his brother Leonardo, of the prestigious architectural firm of Morales and Cia. He was very familiar with the "Garden Cities of Tomorrow" movement that advocated limiting growth of the inner city. Design of the Reparto Miramar was Havana's first departure from the Spanish Urban Ordinances. City blocks were no longer square, but rectangular: approximately 688 by 320 feet. The narrow side of the block always faced the Avenida's east-west orientation, creating a higher market value for those lots. The new socioeconomic use of residential land was well defined by the urban design of Miramar.

Céspedes had the goal of extending the Malecón east toward the beaches, which were a popular destination for summer recreation. This goal was not possible because of the opposition of landowners who preferred to develop First Avenue as a residential street. He was, however, successful in creating Quinta Avenida (Fifth Avenue) as the most prestigious address of Havana. Pedroso's urban plan used Quinta Avenida as the urban generator of Miramar and the most important connection to El Vedado.

Luis Morales y Pedroso included in his plan regulations for setbacks, uses, and materials, along with other restrictions, all of which were common in U.S. cities at that time. Miramar created a new typology of residential subdivisions in Cuba. In association with a group of wealthy investors, Céspedes decided to develop the waterfront at the end of Quinta Avenida, and in June 1917 obtained the approval to build a new *reparto*, the Parque de Diversiones y Residencias (Park of Recreation and Residences). The new subdivision was near the Habana Yacht Club, the first private beach club (founded in 1886).

The new *reparto* at the end of Quinta Avenida was a success. Here the developers hired the American architectural firm of Schultze and Weaver to design La Concha Beach Club in 1928. This firm also designed two superb works of architecture: the Jockey Club and the Gran Casino Nacional (now unfortunately demolished) in

Miramar—a beautiful residential parklike neighborhood
with an abundance of trees and shade.

the same year. Schultze and Weaver were well known among the wealthy Cubans who traveled frequently to New York because they were the designers of the world-renowned and prestigious Waldorf-Astoria Hotel.

La Playa de Marianao, as it was generally known—with its restaurants, bars, nightclubs, and summer hotels—became a popular destination after 1915 when the streetcar system reached the area. The urban vision of Céspedes and the designs of architect Morales y Pedroso changed the urban structure of Havana, creating a new model for the city's future growth. As it grew in the first half of the twentieth century, Havana continued to be one of the most diverse cities in its housing types and urban development in Latin America. This particular model was the continuation of the trend to emulate the suburban lifestyle and architecture found at this time in the United States. Wealthy Habaneros basically left the center colonial city and their Spanish colonial mansions, which often combined commercial and residential use and centered internally on the large, landscaped patio, and instead built homes that were set in the center of the lot and surrounded by open gardens that blended with their neighbors and became part of the neighborhood landscape. These neighborhoods were beautiful in themselves at the expense of the privacy, density, and serenity of the original Spanish colonial home.

Urban Growth during the Tumultuous 1950s

During the first half of the twentieth century, Havana grew from the central city to the affluent western residential neighborhoods discussed above. This growth was facilitated by the relative ease of transit on the Malecón and Quinta Avenida to the city center. The scene of rapid growth then moved in the 1950s back to El Vedado and the area off the Malecón around the Hotel Nacional. But first a little background.

The tumultuous times of the 1950s made Havana the tourists' tropical paradise, the fun destination of the world. Attracted by a wide-open city of prostitution, bars, nightclubs, lavish shows, gambling, and glamorous hotels, all peppered with film stars and celebrities, tourism, which had started in the 1930s, blossomed in the 1950s.

At the same time there was political mayhem. In 1952 Fulgencio Batista staged a coup and became the country's dictator. The Batista government then brought to Havana American racketeers: notorious gangsters such as Charles "Lucky" Luciano, Santos Trafficante, and the mastermind of it all, Meyer Lansky. They, in turn, brought Las Vegas and Miami to Havana, and with them large and garish hotels and lavish casinos.

This was the time when the modern architecture of the International Style and its derivatives was putting its stamp on the world, and such buildings soon arrived on Havana's shores—clean, simple, white concrete boxes devoid of all detail and showing their age quickly in the hot tropical sun and salty sea air. This became the accepted style for most modern buildings in Havana.

Important buildings constructed at this time were the Bus Station (1949), Palace of Justice (1957), José Martí National Library (1957), National Lottery (1958), National Theater (1960), Havana City Hall (1960), Municipal Palace (1960), and Ministry of Transport (1961).[2] At the same time, the old city center had areas of slums with dilapidated rooming houses and tenements, with many families sharing an interior court for all their basic services, including hanging clothes to dry. In 1960 the planner José Luis Sert designed a radical "celebrity" plan for Habana Vieja and the Malecón that would have destroyed the heart of the city. But luckily for the city, it was never executed.[3]

In 1952 the Condominium Law allowed for the first time buildings taller than six stories to be built in Vedado around the National Hotel. This was to accommodate the surge of tourism, and it dramatically changed the city's skyline, destroying its harmonious horizontality while blocking the sky, the breeze, and the vistas to the sea. Modern hotels filled this new void with the building of the Habana Riviera, Havana Hilton (1958, later named the Habana Libre), and many more.

In 1993 a Spanish group built the twenty-two-story Hotel Melin-Cohiba, which towers over the already huge Hotel Havana Hilton. With an ugly metal and reflective glass facade, it was designed, like the other hotels, completely out of scale and character with the human and harmonious city, an early example or warning of what modern architecture can bring to a wonderful city.

Gran Casino Nacional—located in the Marianao neighborhood. The fountain (*The Nymphs*) in front of the building was part of the original Gran Casino Nacional designed by Rafael Goyeneche, a Mexican architect. The building was extensively remodeled in 1928 by American architects Schultze and Weaver, the architects of the Waldorf-Astoria Hotel in New York City. When the Grand Nacional Casino was demolished in 1959, the fountain was relocated in front of what is now the Tropicana. The fountain was designed in 1920 by sculptor Aldo Gamba.

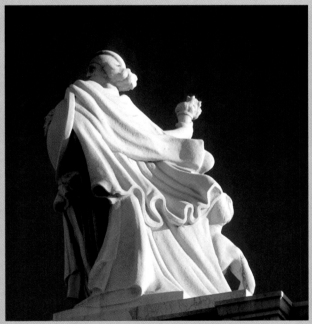

Monument to honor José Miguel Gómez (1936), one of the initiators of the Ten Years' War (1868–1878) and Cuba's first president in arms (1909–1913), Avenida de los Presidentes, principal street of El Vedado. This monument was designed by Giovanni Nicolini, an Italian, and the marble for the project was imported from Italy. The design precedent was highly criticized by Italians, who called it the wedding cake because of its similarity to the Victor Emmanuel Monument (Il Vottoriano) in Piazza Venezia, Rome (1885–1911). The landscape of Avenida de los Presidentes was designed by Jean Claude Nicolas Forestier. The concept of a residential street having a monument of this grandeur and beauty is a testament to the vision of Havana's planners.

A handsome Havana apartment building overlooking a tranquil park. The one discordant note is the subtle bit of government propaganda found in Fidel Castro's public display of a tank—a symbol of war and conflict and a warning that Big Brother is always watching.

Typical 1930s residence in Central Habana. Its rational, modern International Style is a paradox of unadorned architectonic rectangles, boxes, and voids. White concrete is the entire palette. Oh, to have the cool solitude and beauty of a lushly landscaped Spanish enclosed patio with its fountain and all the adorning details.

Architectural diversity in Central Habana. This photograph reveals the visual conflict that occurs when many architects work independently without concern for their neighbors, neighborhood, or the totality of the city. Angles, glancing geometry, and various styles all compete for space, for their "day in the sun." But then suddenly, rising above the fray, is the pure flame of modernity—the architectural phallic symbol of the International Style—to save the day.

El Capitolio Nacional, as seen from Parque de la Fraternidad. Forestier's plan for the national capitol gave Havana gracious public spaces and powerful symbolic architecture based on a rational order and a fine sense of urban beauty.

Part IV

Influences and Important Landmarks

Chapter 10

Urbanism, Culture, and Art in the Cuban Republic

Proposed system for avenues and parks in greater Habana by Jean Claude Nicolas Forestier.

Plan for University City by Jean Claude Nicolas Forestier.

The Planner, Jean Claude Nicolas Forestier

Jean Claude Nicolas Forestier (1861–1930), the commissioner of gardens of Paris and conservator of the promenades, was an architect, landscape designer, and town planner. He designed gardens in France, Spain, Morocco, and Portugal, and created designs relating to urban and landscape planning in Buenos Aires before he worked in Havana.

Forestier was brought to Havana in 1925 to design a new vision for the city in keeping with its fresh position as a potentially great capital of a new republic. To fully appreciate Forestier's urban work in Havana, one should understand briefly his previous work and urban landscape philosophy.

In France, Forestier developed an arboretum at Vincennes as well as the gardens of the Champs-de-Mars located below the Eiffel Tower. In 1925 he became inspector of gardens for the International Exhibition of Decorative Arts. In Spain, he designed the Parque de María Luisa in Seville and the Parc de la Ciutadella and Laribal Gardens in Barcelona, dating to the International Exposition of Barcelona in 1929.

In the Laribal Gardens, which Forestier designed for Montjuïc, Barcelona, he combined multiple styles—the Mediterranean tradition, Catalan culture, the concepts of the Arabian gardens of the Iberian Peninsula, and the gardens of the Generalife at the Alhambra in Granada. His work in Barcelona employed brilliant use of ceramic tile, ornamental water fountains, and reflection pools.[1]

Also designed by Forestier, the Parque de María Luisa in Seville was created for the Ibero-American Exposition of 1929. Even today a carriage ride through this park is an Old World experience. Its Plaza de España is a wonderful example of the historic/romantic style, where the traditions of Arabic and Andalusian art are combined with fine craftsmanship and harmonious design to create wondrous architecture. It fronts onto a public plaza and semicircular canal, where small boats offer a tranquil ride to a bygone age. Combining this architecture with formal landscaped geometry—the opposite of the picturesque tradition—conveys something of the flavor of Chicago's World's Columbian Exposition of 1893, designed by another urban landscape poet, Frederick Law Olmsted (1822–1903).[2]

Forestier was called upon to come to Havana to help design a capital befitting the new republic. He visited Havana three times with a team of French professionals between 1925 and 1930. In Havana, he developed his desire to create a bond between

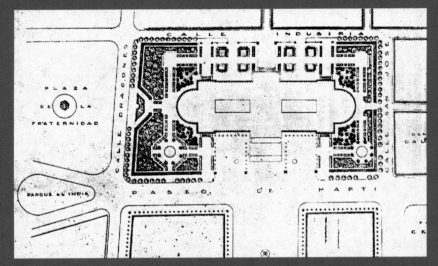

Plan for the Jardínes del Capitolio by Jean Claude Nicolas Forestier.

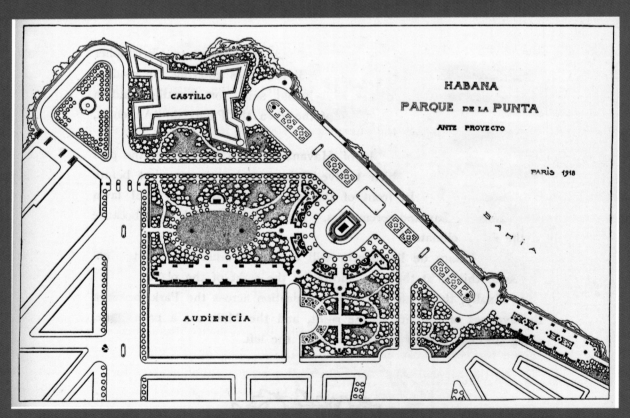

Plan for a park at La Punta (1918) by Jean Claude Nicolas Forestier.

the city and its urban landscape, just as he had done in Paris's suburban ring and in Spain, Morocco, Portugal, and Argentina—namely, in his words, the science of gardens at the service of urban art.[3]

Forestier championed the city as a large urban garden, with public parks and parkways, both small and large, as an essential part of any great city. For Havana, he designed many conceptual plans—some realized, some not—as a general plan of Havana and its vicinity. He designed a grand "Staircase to Príncipe" at the end of Avenida de la Independencia and a grand parkway for Avenida de la Ermita (both unrealized). He also designed the superb master plan for the new campus of La Universidad de la Habana.

Of those concepts that were never executed, one of Forestier's most interesting concerned the existing Malecón. In 1918 Forestier planned a public park creating an unrealized grand entrance to the Castillo de San Salvador de la Punta, which anchors the Malecón. This park would have consisted of a series of geometrically terraced gardens that poetically acted as theoretical lookouts for approaching vessels to the Bay of Havana, providing a spiritual connection between Havana and the sea.

Forestier designed the landscape plans on the Malecón for monuments at the Plaza del Maine and for Avenida de los Presidentes, one of the most charming, spacious, linear residential parks in the Americas. He designed the Jardínes del Capitolio (Capitol Gardens), which set the landscape framework for the Capitolio and has made it an important symbolic architectural monument fitting naturally into the fabric of Havana. The Jardínes del Capitolio is the primary link between the Parque de la Fraternidad and Parque Central, in keeping with Forestier's concept of a city as a continuous urban garden for the enjoyment of all its citizens.

Catalonian Influences in Havana

Havana has had many flirtations with other cities, mainly Seville and Cádiz, in its long history, but probably the most interesting was its love affair with Catalonia and its capital, Barcelona, in the nineteenth century. The connection between Barcelona and Havana is an important story in the unique urban development of the city.

Much of the wealth that supported architect Antonio Gaudí (1852–1926), the genius of Barcelona, had its origins in the West Indies. In the middle of the nineteenth century, with the Industrial Revolution in full swing, many Catalans, especially those from Barcelona, ventured to the New World to make their fortunes in Spain's Caribbean colonies: Cuba, Puerto Rico, and Santo Domingo. Having absorbed

Plan for University City by Jean Claude Nicolas Forestier.

Paving design and embellishments proposed for the Plaza de la Catedral by Jean Claude Nicolas Forestier.

Miramar—Havana's Garden City.

Miramar—a gentle urban landscape.

much of the Caribbean's flavor in the process, these industrialists returned to Spain with a newly acquired wealth, which many invested in Catalonia. Members of this new class of bourgeoisie with West Indian trappings enjoyed the Caribbean culture and became known as Americanos or Indianos. They were interested in reproducing the atmosphere of the Caribbean in Catalonia. To this day, fishermen along the Catalan coast sing songs called *habaneras*, inspired by remembrances of Havana. Gaudí came into contact with the Americanos, including his clients Antonio López, Eusebio Güell, and Roser Segimon, whose first husband was an Americano.

Gazing on Gaudí's fantastic landscape of forms, there seems to be certain allusions and references to the Caribbean. Whether founded by a direct, historical influence by Gaudí or by coincidence, people see them nonetheless. Another reference to the Caribbean could be inferred from the sculpted stone columns supporting one of the viaducts in Gaudí's Barcelona Parc Güell. One clearly depicts a washerwoman with a blanket on her head who almost seems to sing a Caribbean song.

The strongest connection between the Caribbean and Gaudí came through his patron of forty years, Eusebio Güell I Bacigalupi. Eusebio's father, Joan Güell I Ferrer (1800–1872), an Indiano and the inventor of cotton corduroy, initially made his fortune in textiles in the West Indies in the 1830s. Eusebio was taken on a trip to the Caribbean by his father and later returned to Cuba, where he started his own textile firm. He later carried on the business tradition in Barcelona.[4] Güell became Gaudí's patron in 1878, a relationship that endured until Güell's death in 1918. During this time, Gaudí became Güell's exclusive architect, having entree to the vastly rich society of Güell's peers, many of whom, like Güell himself, were wealthy through some Caribbean connection.

The Industrial Revolution came to Catalonia primarily upon the return from Spanish America of various spirited citizens, especially those in the textile industry. Although Catalans are known as an industrious people with a strong work ethic, Catalonia did not enjoy the same prosperity as did the rest of Spain following Columbus's discovery of America. Spain concentrated on the Americas and forgot the Mediterranean. Ships coming from the Americas, particularly Havana, the backbone of colonial Spain's commerce, were authorized to go to the harbors of Seville or Cádiz, but were not permitted to use the harbor of Catalonia's capital city, Barcelona. In the middle of the eighteenth century, however, King Carlos III liberalized commerce, opening up these harbors and thereby initiating the renaissance of Catalonia in Havana.

Parc Güell, Barcelona, Spain, by Catalonian architect Antonio Gaudí. This park was originally a suburban development by Eusebio Güell, whose family made its fortune in Cuba.

After the Spanish War of Succession (1701–1714), Philip V, grandson of Louis XIV, centralized the organization of Spain, keeping for himself all the privileges then existing in the different regions and kingdoms within the Spanish dominion. As a result, Catalonia could stop vying for privilege and was free to make great progress, particularly in becoming influential in the building of booming Havana.

Throughout the Western world at this time, coupled with the destruction of the medieval city walls, including Havana's, we see the beginning of the evolution of town planning. Barcelona had its Cerdà Plan (by Ildefons Cerdà), which was quite revolutionary and, in part, copied in Havana. As in Barcelona, the corners of all new buildings at each of Havana's street intersections had to be clipped off or beveled to create a small plaza at each intersection. At the same time Havana expanded, Barcelona had its Ensanche, led by architect Antonio Gaudí.

In the words of Juan Bassegoda Nonell, the director of the Royal Gaudí Chair, Polytechnical University of Catalonia, "All of Gaudí's architecture is created by these intuitive, elemental methods, which permitted him to achieve equilibrated forms very like those found in nature."[5] See the natural forms on the exquisite sculptural architecture in Parc Güell, Barcelona.

With the expansion into the new land outside the former walls, Havana became a fertile environment within which architectural passions could bloom. There was a new enthusiasm for building and development among Catalonian industrialists coming to Havana from Barcelona. There was also a revolution in building fuelled by marvelous new materials, good municipal planning, and powerful patrons with new sugar wealth who were interested in building a beautiful Havana and, eventually, a new republic.

Catalonians brought their long tradition of craftsmanship to Havana. Since medieval times, Catalonia has produced excellent carpenters, stonecutters, brick masons, locksmiths, printers, painters, and stained-glass craftsmen, a Catalonian trademark. Havana formed a fruitful ground for architecture, with a strong affinity for handicraft and integral ornamentation. One example is the shape and surrounds of the upper sections of the Bacardí Building that are pure "Catalonia Modernismo."

Twentieth-Century Influence of Society and Art

The nineteenth century brought the end of Havana's colonial aristocracy and the birth of a prosperous, modern middle class. This broader spectrum of wealthy society had a thirst for the latest fashion, design, sports, architecture, and just plain old-fashioned gossip and found it in the richly illustrated pages of one spectacular magazine, *Social*. *Social* was the creation in 1916 of Conrado Walter Massaguer, an illustrator and caricaturist who captured the social life of the city until 1937. During this time, *Social* was an important work of popular avant-garde Cuban art, bringing to Havana the clean flat surfaces and colors of Japanese prints, the designs of Art Deco, and the delicacy of craft of the legendary English illustrator Aubrey Beardsley, all dedicated to the wonderful life of pleasure.

SOCIAL

VOLUMEN VI.
AGOSTO, 1921.

CONRADO W. MASSAGUER
DIRECTOR

NUMERO 8
40 CENTAVOS

SOCIAL

VOL. IV. NO. 10
OCTUBRE, 1919
30 CENTAVOS

SOCIAL

CONRADO W. MASSAGUER

La Quinta de los Molinos.

Chapter 11

Landmarks of Havana: Symbolic Architecture in a Historic Environment

La Quinta de los Molinos.

La Quinta de los Molinos

In 1837 Governor Miguel Tacón decided to build a summer residence outside of Havana on a site at the end of the Military Paseo, later called Paseo de Tacón and then Paseo de Carlos III. The site was located just outside the military perimeter of the Castillo del Príncipe, the largest fortress outside of Havana.

The modest house was built with local materials—some left over from other government projects—but soon Governor Tacón decided to upgrade La Quinta de los Molinos (The Country House near the Mills). It acquired this name because of two mills located nearby. The remodeling and enlargement of the house were designed by architect Carrillo de Albornoz in an effort to make the summer residence competitive with the luxurious villas of El Cerro. The largest portion of the site had extensive tropical gardens and barracks for the governor's personal guards. Most of the vegetation for this botanical garden and its elaborate iron garden fence had to be relocated to the site since the site was originally used as the location of the first railroad terminal, the Villanueva station.

La Quinta was used as residence of General Máximo Gómez, head of the Cuban Revolutionary Army, after the War of Independence, and a few years later it was annexed to the National University as part of the Facultad de Agronomía.

Today La Quinta is a museum dedicated to the memory of General Máximo Gómez. It has an interesting collection of furniture, and the windows are remarkable examples of color glass works. The gardens maintain a charming character as a tropical botanical garden.

Palacio Presidencial

The Palacio Presidencial (now the Museo de la Revolución), is framed by Avenida de las Palmas (or Avenida de las Misiones, just outside the original Old City walls) and occupies an entire square block, one street from Paseo del Prado and therefore part of the Prado's neighborhood. This neoclassical palace, designed by Cuban architect Rodolfo Maruri and Belgian architect Paul Belau—Belau also designed the Palacio del Centro Gallego and the Gran Teatro de la Habana—is a grand and imposing symbol of the power and majesty of Cuba as a new republic. Inaugurated in 1920 by President Mario García Menocal, the palace was the residence of twenty-

Palacio Presidencial (1919), designed by Paul Belau and Rodolfo Maruri, Habana Vieja
(now the Museo de la Revolución).

one Cuban presidents prior to the Communist revolution in 1959. The interiors have elements designed by the legendary Louis Comfort Tiffany, America's premier designer of the day.

The commanding feature of this palace is its glass-tiled dome dominating its Prado neighborhood. This beautifully proportioned dome crowns the building in a way that seems to symbolize the new Cuban republic as the crowns of Spanish royalty once symbolized colonial rule over Cuba. Located directly over the grand staircase, the interior of the dome has a circular and radiating ceramic design that accentuates the drama of this monumental space. The light from the dome's clerestory vertically pierces the building's interiors, culminating at the grand staircase below. This symmetrical and marble grand staircase leads up to the Salón de los Espejos, with its front terrace commanding a fine view of the Bay of Havana. The main reception hall has a frescoed ceiling by Cuban painters Armado Menocal and Antonio Rodríquez Morey and is lined with large mirrors (*espejos*) similar to those that grace the Hall of Mirrors at the Chateau de Versailles (1668) and the Great Hall in Catherine the Great's palace (1752) outside of St. Petersburg, Russia.

Forestier wanted this monumental palace to be a focal point within his plan for the Avenida de las Misiones, which he opened up and created as one of the city's grand public spaces. This stunning public space creates a vista within the city so that the presidential palace could unify, both visually and spiritually, the city with the sea. The palace has the basic characteristic of Havana's architecture, a strong colonnaded base as a solid pronouncement of strength in its deeply shaded arcade. Its facade's upper floors clearly express the formal living and ceremonial spaces within. Large glass windows emphasize the vertical, as do the corner's engaged towers, with their pointed pinnacles silhouetted against the sky. The central grand balcony, even when not in use, indicates a special place for public pronouncements and speeches. Today, a tank from the Communist revolution, raised on a pedestal, is used as a public monument that graces the front of the palace.

La Universidad de la Habana: A Monumental Campus for a Growing City

La Universidad de la Habana was founded in 1728 by papal bull as a pontifical university, the highest rank for an academic institution in the Spanish Empire. Initially the university was located in the Convent of San Juan of Letrán in old Havana.

The university was relocated to its present location in 1902 by initiative of the great Cuban educator Enrique José Varona, first secretary of education of the new republic. The army had used the site for storage, and the existing warehouses were adapted to educational uses.

Top: La Universidad de la Habana. The main entrance staircase (1927) of eighty-eight steps presents the symmetrical and classic planning of the university and its terraced gardens.

Above: The formal and classical Central Library of La Universidad de la Habana.

Top: This building at La Universidad de la Habana displays a classical dignity for higher education.

Above: A landscaped courtyard at La Universidad de la Habana carries the Spanish architectural tradition.

At La Universidad de la Habana, the statue of the Alma Mater (Mario Korbel, 1919) is the focal point at the top of the grand stairway.

The university campus was redeveloped through a slow process of changes and improvements. The emergence of the present-day campus continued in 1916 when President Mario García Menocal commissioned Cuban artist Emilio Heredia to design the entrance and front part of the campus.

Heredia proposed a public park as the transitional element to the city, followed by an urban complex that featured a monumental set of stairs that dominated the site by virtue of its a central location. The stairs were flanked by two large pavilions and culminated in a classical entrance. Heredia created the precedent for the present-day campus, in spite of the fact that his proposal was never implemented.

The great stairs of the university were designed by Cuban architects Raúl Otero and César Guerra, with the cooperation of a French team of advisers. The entrance culminates with the portico designed by architect Enrique Martinez. The buildings at both sides of the entrance were designed by the Cuban architects Luis Duval and Pedro Martínez Inclán. This completed the entrance to the university, similar to Heredia's original proposal in 1916.

Another component of the university was the hospital Universitario General Calixto García. Constructed during the administration of President Menocal, it began with a commitment in 1918 to build the largest and best public hospital in Cuba on a site next to the campus.

The campus included a plaza defined by well-designed buildings. One of them is the library designed by Joaquín E. Weiss, while another is the Sciences Building designed by Pedro Martínez Inclán. The dominant feature of the campus and part of the image of the university is the statue *Alma Mater* by Czech sculptor Mario Korbel. The statue was initially placed in the center of the campus plaza (today called Plaza Cadenas). Forestier suggested relocating it to the present location, thereby dominating the entrance to the campus.

Another process in the planning of the university was Forestier's proposed development plan for the city. The plan was presented to Cuban authorities during his second visit to Havana in 1928. Most of the proposals, such as avenues, parkways, and gardens, required the extensive demolition and expropriation of many private properties. The plan was never seriously considered due to Cuba's economic crisis at the time. Rector José Cadenas did, however, implement some aspects of Forestier's plan.

Today La Universidad de la Habana, the first university founded in the Americas, is an urban landmark in the city and a leading academic institution in Cuba.

El Cementerio de Colón: A City within a City

El Cementerio de Colón (Necrópolis de Colón, Columbus Cemetery), named after Cristóbal Colón (Christopher Columbus), is one of the remarkable works of art within Havana that sets the city apart from almost all the other great cities of the world. Here Habaneros commemorate death as a celebration of life. Only on a few occasions did great civilizations memorialize in their architecture the most common (along with birth) of human experiences, death. The greatest of all were the ancient Egyptians, whose mortuary temples and great pyramids created a lasting tribute of respect and homage to their fallen ancestors. A more modest but equally unique artistic expression of a society's ancestral homage are the giant stone sculptures of the prehistoric people of Easter Island in the Pacific. However, with few exceptions, cemeteries generally are not important expressions of a city's art and are relegated to unimportant locations within the community.

Such was not the case in Havana, where a rare and important artistic tribute was paid to its dead in the creation of El Cementerio de Colón. The city's tribute to its dead is a sculpture garden of incredible beauty and intensity. It is reminiscent of the density of art in the Prado Museum in Madrid or the Hermitage Museum in St. Petersburg. Art is everywhere, and therefore it is nowhere. The entire scene is transformed into an integrated whole, one giant piece of a remarkable sculptural montage.

Usually sculpture gardens distribute distinctive works of sculpture sparsely within their landscaped boundaries. But in El Cementerio de Colón, the sculptural tombs—of all qualities, styles, materials, sizes, and relative importance—are mixed into one unified work of sculptural art. This cemetery is a work of art in its own right. Its layout is a plan of a city with a proper monumental entrance, the Puerta de la Paz (Gate of Peace), and a central focal point at the intersection of its main cross streets—the small but elegant Romanesque-Byzantine chapel. This "city of the dead" comes to life when mourners slowly walk in procession beside a floral-bedecked car through the rows of memories to the Habaneros who preceded them on their inevitable journey. A prayer and hymn are given in the chapel, and the mourners then walk to a rhythmical cadence, ending at the final resting place.

The design of this landmark cemetery was the result of a competition won by architect Calixto de Loira, who was then named construction director of the project. The *primera piedra* (cornerstone) for the new cemetery was placed on October 30, 1871, with the construction starting the following month.

The winning design was developed following the strict Ordinances for Catholic Cemeteries adopted during Pope Gregory I's reign in the sixth century. The ordinances required a layout consisting of five crosses. The primary cross was defined

El Cementerio de Colón—Puerta de la Paz, by Calixto de Loira and Eugenio Rayneri (1871).

Top: El Cementerio de Colón—Capilla Central, octagonal chapel, the focal point of the cemetery.

Above: A funeral procession in 1997.

Top: El Cementerio de Colón—tomb of Catalina Lasa (1936) by René Lalique, turn-of-the-century French Art Deco sculptor, painter, and designer of jewelry and glass.

Above: Tomb of José F. Mata (1920).

Top: El Cementerio de Colón—tomb of the Falla Bonet family.

Above: The interior of the family tomb of the international and Cuban architect Andres Duany.

by the two main avenues: one north-south from the main gate of the cemetery to the end, and another avenue oriented east-west in the middle of the site. A plaza marked the crossing of the two avenues. De Loira was successful in incorporating the five crosses requirement found in a typical ancient Roman city. The main cross produced four sections, and inside each section the same pattern of avenues was created to form a cross of a second order, also with a plaza of smaller size at the crossing point.

Originally the tombs were assigned according to the social status (defined by a church committee) of the deceased, but this procedure was abandoned in the new republic.

Architect de Loira's plan also followed the construction ordinances adopted by the city of Havana in 1861. Lohania Aruca, a Cuban architectural historian, considered that de Loira's project took into account the most modern ideas of Spanish and French urbanism, represented by Ildefons Cerdà in Barcelona and Baron Haussmann in Paris.[1]

Initially the tombs were very simple in construction, utilizing local materials and without much distinction, but when the economic conditions of Cuba improved at the beginning of twentieth century, the tombs became more detailed and elaborate. Italian artisans living in Havana dedicated to selling marble from Carrara in Italy and other parts of Europe became interested in building funerary monuments. Many Cuban organizations such as professional and commercial associations decided to build funerary monuments to honor their deceased members. Governments also decided to honor patriots and leaders, and soon the image of the cemetery changed.

In the late 1920s wealthy families started building elaborate monuments designed by well-known architects and designers using an abundance of sculpture, rich and exotic materials, and a variety of architectural forms.

The expressive and sometimes extravagant tombs were not always recognized as being architecturally significant by some architects and writers. Pedro Martínez Inclan, in his book *Havana Actual* (1925), wrote about the cemetery, "Colón Cemetery is a little pagan, despite the fact that it is full of saints and crosses."[2]

The cemetery is a monument that encompassed an architectural and artistic cross section of values and attitudes of Cuban society covering more than a century. The characteristics of El Cementerio de Colón are very well presented in an article by architect Enrique Martínez, reproduced in the book *Cuba, Architecture and Urbanism*.[3]

Estación Terminal de Trenes

An architectural symbol of Havana's new beginning as a twentieth-century republic is its Estación Terminal de Trenes (Central Railway Station), built where the city's arsenal once stood and designed by the famous New York architect Kenneth McKenzie Murchison (1872–1939). It was completed in 1912 and is still in use today.

It is an imposing, stately building combining the grand symmetry and classicism of the beaux arts movement and the traditional Spanish Renaissance. At the time, the beaux arts style was fashionable in the United States, and therefore in Havana, because of the well-publicized success of the Chicago World's Columbian Exposition of 1893. The combination of these two influences resulted in the National Romantic Style that combined both national folk art and symbolism, in this case related to the Spanish roots of Havana, and the romanticism of the nineteenth-century aesthetic movement (aestheticism). The word "National" refers to regionalism (local or national in embellishments), as opposed to international, the worldly phenomenon of Art Nouveau, Art Deco, and the International Style, all without reference to folk traditions, mores, or customs. The word "Romantic" refers to the picturesque and poetic. The most famous example of this National Romantic Style was later to be Stockholm's City Hall (1923), where the Nobel Prize is annually presented.

The Estación Central de Ferrocarriles's facade is symmetrical about the main lobby flanked on either side by the baggage room and the café. The twin towers, one with the shield of Cuba and the other with the shield of Havana, recall the fifteenth-century La Giralda's bell tower in Seville and contain the station's utilitarian spaces. Railroads and the steam engine changed the nineteenth-century world and Cuba's as well. This symbol of the future rose above Havana as a beacon of the city's emerging modern era.

The Bacardí Building

The story of the Bacardí Building begins with an appreciation of Cuban rum, which started in the early 1500s with the distillation and fermentation of sugarcane. In colonial times, particularly in the nineteenth century, Cuba was a world leader in the exportation of three agricultural products grown on slave-labor plantations: sugar, tobacco, and rum. As the world became addicted to them, wealth flowed into Cuba through the port of Havana, where most of the shipments originated.

Cuban culture is based, in part, on its music, but these rhythms receive considerable help from the effects of rum, especially for fiestas and festivals, or as an offering to the *orishas* (gods) of the Santeria, also called Regla de Ocha. Santeria is the African-Catholic religion started by the Yoruba slaves from Nigeria that forms an

Estación Terminal de Trenes (Central Railroad Station) (1912). Architect: Kenneth McKenzie Murchison.

interesting part of Cuban culture. This religion blends Catholicism with an animistic spirituality whose priests and priestesses (*santeros* and *santeras*) mix African and Latin music, rhythms, costumes, and dance into an exciting spiritual art.[4]

In 1829 a Spanish emigrant with an inventive mind and love for drink, Don Facundo Bacardí Masó, settled in Santiago, Cuba. He soon discovered that the native and popular rum was dark and thick, and often had a distasteful flavor. He experimented with the fermentation and distillation process and discovered that if the rum was charcoal filtered, the impurities would be eliminated, and a light, smooth, flavorful drink resulted. The rest is history.

In 1862 Bacardí created a tin-roofed distillery with a colony of fruit bats in the roof. In Cuban mythology, the fruit bat brings good luck and is Bacardí's symbol to this day. It flies proudly on the top pinnacle of the company's former Havana headquarters in Central Habana.[5] From that small beginning, Bacardí has become one of the largest suppliers of alcoholic spirits in the world.

Bacardí rum has always supported outstanding architecture throughout the world. The company's Miami, Florida, headquarters—a tall tower glazed with large ceramic murals of giant blue flowers—and its companion low museum encrusted with walls of stained glass are wonderful examples of the International Style in form, yet with the exuberance of the tropics making them a unique and important work of architectural art.

In this tradition, Barcardí's Havana headquarters, built in 1930, was conceived by the Bacardí family, which still owns the company, as their contribution to the state of fine architecture. Its designers—Esteban Rodríguez Castells, Rafael Fernández Ruenes, and José Menéndez—won the commission to design a building fundamentally in the style of the pioneer nineteenth-century Chicago Style—a vertical, tall office building—of which Louis Sullivan's St. Louis Wainwright Building (1891) and his Chicago Auditorium Building (1889) were early and historic examples. The architects, after visiting Paris during its Art Deco building period, added integral decoration in the geometric Art Deco style plus exterior folk art embellishments that have Catalonian Modernismo form, materials, and construction techniques, particularly in the top story's window shapes, fretwork grills, and brickwork (see chapter 10). The decorations of idealized women, a popular Art Nouveau motif, were glazed with a rich terracotta finish, while the building's top ziggurat profile, popular in North Africa, silhouettes wonderfully against Havana's clear tropical sky.

There are many typical Art Deco buildings in Havana: the Lopez Serrano Building by Ricardo Mira and Miquel Rosich (1932), the Julio Tarafa residence in Miramar (1933), and the Lalique Mausoleum for Catalina Lasa in El Cementerio de Colón (1936), to name a few.

The Bacardí Building, in total, is an example of a building caught in a transitional period of styles, which at the beginning of the twentieth century often resulted in what can be called the National Romantic Style: a combination of indigenous, symbolic art and a love affair with rich, luxurious materials. The Estación Central de Ferrocarriles is also in that style but with a more Spanish bent. Havana's Nacional Hotel de Cuba, whose basic design is that of the 1920s Florida resort hotels, adds Art Deco embellishments to its roof, parapet, and tower.

The interior public spaces of the Bacardí Building combine these same eclectic styles with classical columns, Art Deco geometry, and applied art of marble and stainless steel. The vestibule has inverted stepped forms that draw the visitor to the elevators, originally clad with a radiant sun design, a common element adapted by Art Deco from the ancient Egyptians. The two-story exhibition hall has wonderful Art Deco chandeliers and, combined with the mezzanine bar, creates one simple interplay of architectonic space.

To summarize the landmarks of Havana is difficult, for so much of its architectural treasures, both large and small, could be considered landmarks. Havana's important structures have been outstanding examples of the various evolving architectural styles that were admired during the various historic periods of their times. Havana seemed to always be on the forefront of architectural design in almost all its historic periods. While many countries in South America and Central America, and particularly the Caribbean, were often stagnant in their architectural development, Havana seemed to produce jewels. In contemporary times, even with almost untold wealth, many cities still have not built the classic examples of architecture that Havana has. Havana seemed to have possessed that rare quality of taste and desire to create the right thing at the right time. Unfortunately, during the last half of the twentieth century, the city has not produced architectural gems but has let its urban treasures tarnish and disintegrate. With the exception of some spots within the central tourist area, where some government restoration has occurred to mask the city for visitors, the reality is that the city is literally crumbling from neglect.

The Bacardí Building (1930). Architects: Esteban Rodríguez Castells, Rafael Fernández Ruenes, and José Menéndez.

TROPICANA 1997 1939

Part V

A City Infused with the Cuban Spirit

Chapter 12

The Cuban Zest for Life

NO CITY EXISTS IN SECLUSION. To think of a city as purely a collection of architecture or urban spaces, no matter how great or famous, is a distortion of reality. A city is a mirror, and in that mirror is not only the reflection of its built environment but also the image of its people, history, and culture. A city brings buildings together collectively, and only when animated by its citizens does it bring joy and visual excitement to all. To divorce the civilization from its architecture renders the architecture to a position of an unimportant object, isolated and unfulfilled. The manipulation of the elements of a city, its structures and symbols, becomes important only with the impact the city has on the emotions, feelings, and, yes, the memories of its citizens. The test of a great city is how it is part of and interacts with the other elements of its culture. In only few moments in history have certain people under certain circumstances converged with ideas and ideals that create a superb culture that ultimately emerges and evolves into a great city such as Havana.

To think of Havana, one has to understand the strong Cuban culture in its many forms: Cuban music, Cuban dance, Cuban cuisine, Cubans' strong family ties, and Cubans' zest for life, and even its smallest elements such as a Cuban cigar or the tiny shot of strong Cuban coffee that one can only sip—these are as much a part of Havana as its architectural details or the dry facts of its history. We consider the city from its corner all-night coffee stands to its legendary Cabaret Tropicana; from its vibrant Habaneros who still live in Havana to those in exile throughout the world who all share the passion for all things Cuban; from the city of bright tropical light to the city that loves the night; from those that only tap to the Afro-Cuban beat to those who dance in the shadows, taking small steps to a rhythmical rumba.

Cabaret Tropicana

Havana at night can be summed up in one Oscar Wilde quote: "Life is too important to be taken seriously."

Havana, before the Great Depression, had two casinos associated with its racetrack, Oriental Park, for rich American winter visitors. These did poorly through the Depression. However, in the 1940s Havana again became a city of pleasures, a city of the syncopated rhythm, a city that exemplified the Cuban zest for life. The finest example of this relishing of pleasure was the magical nightclub Cabaret Tropicana, probably the most famous and spectacular nightclub in the world. *Variety* magazine once stated: "Tropicana need not fear of competition from other night-

Cabaret Tropicana, Arcos De Cristal Hall, designed by the architect Max Borges.
Awarded the gold medal by the National College of Architects (1951).

clubs. It could fire the entertainers, ban the musicians and serve milk instead of Scotch and people would still flock to see the place. The club opened on December 30, 1939, and the postcard image of Havana became the Morro Castle, Bacardí Rum and the Tropicana night club."[1]

The Tropicana has flourished under both the American mafia and Fidel Castro, and it is one of the dictator's greatest generators of U.S. dollars. It is located on a nine-acre country estate, of which six acres were covered with a lush tropical garden. Originally this was Villa Mina, a country estate belonging to the wealthy Cuban matron doña Mina Perez Chaumont. Located in the adjoining municipality of Marianao, this charming country mansion and its well-preserved gardens have never been the same since its transformation into the Tropicana.

Originally the main attraction was the open air in the garden, with only the moon and stars above. In those pre-air-conditioning days, outdoor dining and dancing were Caribbean and South Florida traditions. Martin Fox, a man of unusual vision, bought the club in 1939 and made it into the world's most beautiful nightclub.

If you were one of the 1,000 nightly guests, colored lights in the coconut palms, royal palms, and mango trees would greet you as you entered. Then, as you arrived with a sense of anticipation, perhaps a spray of the mist from one of the fountains would filter across the walk. Through this cool mist you would see a small reflection pool and the *Dance of the Hours*, a sculpture by Rita Longo of a stylized Art Deco ballerina gracefully dancing over mirrored water (once located at the Gran Casino National in Vedado). You would then be greeted by the headwaiter, who was and probably still is today one of the best-paid men in Havana.

Originally in the days of gambling, off the entrance foyer was the sumptuous chandeliered Club Room that made the Tropicana the "Monte Carlo of the Americas." Here the beautiful people sat at a circle of gaming tables surrounding "the pit" and played roulette, dice, blackjack, slots, chemin de fer, and countless other games of luck.

In addition to the club's outdoor dining, dancing, and show areas there was the interior salon, the fabulous Crystal Arch Room. Designed by architect Max Borges Jr., it was a unique work of sculptural architecture with giant soaring crescent slabs suspended in midair, separated by almost-invisible crystal panels allowing the romantic and deliciously lighted tropical gardens to come alive and engulf the space. Dancers danced their magic in the club, on the thin roof arches, and in the trees beyond.

Think of old days and the totality of the night; the slightly revealing gowns and white linen suits of the beautiful patrons; the tuxedos of the croupiers; the deluxe service and French cuisine; the unbelievably dazzling pageants of rhythm and color choreographed by Cuba's famous Roderico "Rodney" Neyra; the headliners

Xavier Cugat, Carmen Miranda, Nat "King" Cole, or Josephine Baker—all cooled by the newly installed air-conditioning—with everybody dancing, for Cubans love to dance, and resonating to the infectious rhythms of the mambo, rumba, or cha-cha.

The Tropicana was a fantasy, a spellbinding kaleidoscope with a cast of over 150—the Afro-Cuban music of three intoxicating bands, one with thirty-two musicians, and swirling, exotic dancers in spectacular costumes precariously balancing huge, feathered headdresses and long poles with lavish props above—while outside the starry night sky fought for attention with the rainbow of bright lights bathing the building and grounds. The tall tropical trees came alive with sudden burst of lights, like giant sunspots, illuminating beautiful showgirls draped high on their branches—the perfect combination of the Caribbean tropics and the legacy of the long-legged Andalusian flamenco dancers—all under the hypnotic spell of a pulsating Latin beat. To appreciate the grandeur of the Tropicana is to visualize just one of its shows where Cuban music and African rhythms were combined into a portrayal of the Omelen-Ko, an African baptism where the frenzied rhythms of the lucami ritual were expressed by the tam-tam Bata drums, and the Illa, Aokonlolo, and Itosteles were all played by members of this African faith.

Habaneros: The People of Havana

Los Habaneros, the people of Havana . . . longing to leave while longing to stay . . . living in magical Havana . . . the drums from Africa, guitars from Andalusia . . . romantic, beautiful women with tight-fitting skirts . . . Santeria, the Catholic Church . . . white Guayabera and linen suits, all starched and pressed . . . broad-brimmed Panama hats, Tranbia Cine, sexuality, *loteria*, cockfights, El Floridita, El Carnaval, bright trumpets, the beat of claves and conga drums, blaring boom boxes, late-night clubs, all-night Cuban coffee stands, the juice of the cane, *café con leche*, *ropa vieja*, *picadillo*, arroz con pollo, paella, spicy roast pork, sweet dark rum, Cuba Libre, baseball, Ballet Nacional de Cuba, quick Spanish, playful children, drinking sweet *batido*, hand-rolled cigars . . . hard-working, bright, warm, expressive, affectionate . . . a people where family ties are strong.

A City of the Night

In the "Roaring Forties," Havana was the fun capital of the world. Many elements were in play heading for a slow collision. Adding to the rich Cuban culture were the wide-open gambling, the last glamour stop of Hollywood's golden age, and the storm clouds of revolution just over the horizon. Many nightclubs opened with

dinner shows and a casino. Havana had over 100 bars and cocktail lounges, plus the 3,000 *badegas* (corner stores) that sold liquor by the bottle or glass. Havana had returned to the good old days of Prohibition, when the city was a haven to revelers with an incurable thirst.

In addition to the Tropicana, two other top nightclubs flourished: the Montmartre, in the city, and the Sans Souci, seven miles outside of Havana. The Sans Souci (an old Spanish countryside villa) was founded after World War I when wealthy Americans traveled to and splurged in Havana. It was one of the top clubs in the world and never completely closed despite the repeal of Prohibition and the Great Depression, when tourism dwindled to a trickle.

Peppering the nightlife with extra dazzle were the performers and celebrities who flocked to Havana: Ava Gardner, Jimmy Durante, Groucho Marx, David Selznick, Marlon Brando, Dorothy Lamour, Maurice Chevalier, Eartha Kitt, Edith Piaf, Cab Calloway, Tony Martin, Ernest Hemingway, to name just a few.

In 1956 Wilbur Clark, who also ran Las Vegas's Desert Inn, opened a casino in the Hotel National, then Havana's largest and finest, with 450 rooms and a garden with views of the ocean. It had the Casino Parisian, the International Casino, and the Starlight Terrace. This icon has been renovated and is still the most elegant hotel in Havana.

Havana's Afro-Cuban Music

Few cities in the world are as well known primarily for their music as Havana is for its Afro-Cuban rhythms, a fusion of African drums, Spanish guitar, and the French minuet. Vienna, Buenos Aires, and New Orleans, the homes of the waltz, tango, and jazz, respectively, are probably the only other great cities where music has so deeply infused itself into a city's culture. Havana is one of these cities where this strange combination of music, architecture, and culture are imbedded into the consciousness of all.

Havana has always been alive with its music. Any two spoons can be stuck together to become claves and used to punctuate a syncopated Latin beat; any two wooden boxes can become bongos; any scratched gourd and stick can be stroked as a *guira*; any window can be opened and, with its curtain billowing, transmit the thunder of a distant boom box with its rhythm of the rumba, mambo, or salsa as it infuses the entire neighborhood.

Afro-Cuban music was born in the sounds of Cuba's national dance, the *danzon*, and was transformed into the exciting mambo, a beat created in Cuba but raised in New York. The *danzon* itself came from an eighteenth-century English country dance, which the French transformed into the *contredanze*. Then Oriente Province gave birth to the *son*, which took Havana by storm in the Roaring Twenties.

The *descargas* (jam sessions/improvisations), reinforced by the radio's broadcasts of American jazz from New Orleans, started Cuban musicians on their quest for a true national music.

Legendary Israel "Cachao" Lopez played in the dance orchestra of flutist Antonio Arcano, Arcano y sus Maravillas, and by adding *descarga* to the *danzonas* morphed the music into the mambo. Cachao and his brother Orestes, a cellist, bassist, and composer, were the fathers of the mambo. Internationally, this rhythm spread by the experiments and big-band sound of pianist and bandleader Damaso Perez Prado. The recording world then stamped the music and Cuba's popular rhythms—*son-montuno*, rumba, bolero, conga, mambo, cha-cha, salsa, and others—into the consciousness of the world. It was infectious music, and Cuba's improvisational style soon infected the world.[2] The song "The Peanut Vendor" started the world dancing the rumba even though it was a *son* and not a true rumba. Celia Cruz was the Cuban singing rage of the 1940s, and Beny Moré, affectionately called "el Beny," was the hottest Cuban singer in the 1940s and 1950s.

In "Archetype, Architecture," the planner and philosopher Edmund N. Bacon stated: "A new understanding of architecture as music is now beginning. Because music depends absolutely on continuity, with no discrete parts that stand alone, it becomes a rigorous taskmaster for architecture, where fragmented parts all too often are seen as objects in their own right. The fragmentation of cities for the ego of architecture is the curse of our day."[3]

So, in addition to its music, Havana's architecture has a unique continuity and musical rhythm of its own, creating a musical composition built in stone.

In Plaza de la Catedral, a communal art show exemplifies animated public spaces in a mixed-use city.

Chapter 13

The Characteristics
of the City

AT THE OUTSET of this chapter concerning the fundamental urban characteristics of Havana, it should be noted that we are discussing the basic time-honored qualities of the city and not the present-day cloud of decay and neglect that covers the city as a dense fog would blanket an otherwise beautiful country scene.

The eminent Cuban architectural historian Eduardo Luis Rodríguez, in his introduction to *Inside Havana*, comments on the paradox between Havana's state of ruin and its resulting urban conservation and form: "The existing patrimony deteriorated to such an extent that many sensitive pieces have been lost and many others are almost unrecognizable and unrecoverable today, while the majority are in urgent need of some sort of constructive intervention. On the other hand, the absence of significant investments over a long period had the secondary effect of preventing the senseless and progressive demolition of valuable works such as what took place in other countries at the same time. This produced the phenomenon of a city preserved in a semi-fossilized state."[1]

A Dynamic, Organic City

Havana is a dynamic city that has always been full of excitement and change, and even though its pace has been slowed considerably by the Communist revolution, it is still alive with its own unique, dynamic rhythm. Its streets are animated by 1940s–1950s Dodges, Chevrolets, Cadillacs, Packards, and Buicks, all surprisingly in working condition, which punctuate the cityscape as colorful works of kinetic art. The ghost of Hemingway still hangs in the shadows, and the artistic culture of Havana is still enjoyed in the graceful choreography of the world-renowned Ballet Nacional de Cuba.

Havana is a magical city with a strange mystical attraction. It is a city of unknown mystical charm; a city possessed; a noble yet occasionally sordid city born of part genius, with a large dose of land speculation.

Those who live in Havana feel a deep affection for their city, almost as a friend. Those who have left as exiles feel an equally strong attraction to remember and some day to return. Nobody is indifferent to its magical charm. Many passions are blindly adversarial and discordant, but all people agree on one common theme: the

Solimar Building—an expressionistic work of modern architecture. Architect: Manuel Copado (1944).

Urban settings, neighborhoods, and works of architectonic art interact almost seamlessly in Havana. Here a simple, classic open-air monument frames the view of its adjoining neighbors, enhancing both. This is another example of the architecture of Havana as an expression of Cuban art, culture, and community.

Havana's buildings resonate within their urban landscape, which in turn reaches out to connect to the life of the city. Many call Havana sacred, expressing the love of the Cuban national spirit. In this aspect, it is impossible to truly separate the culture from the architecture.

The streets of Havana used to be full of urban life—street vendors, strollers, and friends greeting each other with children playing close by. Havana is a dense, mixed-use city that generates cherished memories.

Top: Julio Tarafa residence, Art Deco style, by Angel de Zárraga, Miramar, Marianao, Havana (1933). Upper-story addition by Juan M. Lagomasino (1938).

Above: Hotel Nacional de Cuba. Art Deco embellishments on the parapet and tower become small artistic touches within the tapestry of the city.

wonders of the city. Now let's examine what are the urban characteristics that make Havana so extraordinary.

Havana is an organic city with many dimensions, with specks of light and dabs of color like those found on a beautifully feathered parrot, with urban details that make it a textural canvas of an Impressionist painter. Aesthetically, the surface of the city radiates a spontaneous yet organic order rather than the chaos often found in the self-centered contemporary city. Havana synthesizes its many abstractions into a single hard to define but meaningful distinct image.

Havana is not a static city, but a fluid one where people animate its dynamic streetscape. Havana is made up of places for camaraderie and convenience, in sun and shade, private and public, new and old. This montage of urban activities paints its portrait.

Havana is a dense city, one that is concentrated in its core and relative close-in neighborhoods, not the victim of vast urban sprawl. Havana is a carefully thrown fishnet that captures its various urban images in one snapshot, images that are framed by shade trees and period facades, while distant monuments enhance the perspective. Then, when you are aware of this the distant cityscape, you are pulled to the next experience with a wonderful sense of anticipation as your curiosity is aroused and you want to see what is beyond.

A pedestrian network links Havana together in a viable pattern of interaction and human intercourse. The pedestrian is paramount, and the city enjoys a pedestrian scale. Many contemporary cities are consumed by the noise, congestion, and speed of the automobile that creates the impersonal city. Havana, devoid at present of the crushing abundance of automobiles, has a serenity that transcends its size and space. This is due to the consequence of a totalitarian system and not because of any great planning concepts or foresight. This unplanned consequence creates a city where the automobile is not dominant—a human city where the pedestrian moves at a slow pace with time to enjoy the city's historic past.

Cities should be thought of in human terms, not only because they reflect the sum of their inhabitants' lives but also because cities take on human characteristics. Cities can be comfortable and handsome, harmonious and tranquil, kind and interesting, picturesque and grand. Cities have life cycles that ebb and flow like the oceans and their tides. Havana has had this constant rhythm of good and bad, victory and defeat, and hopefully soon, once again, it will emerge from the darkness.

Cities have a collective memory that is a mirror reflecting, in a polished clarity, the sum of the lives of those who inhabit it.

Havana is a holistic city of varying architectural and historic styles as well as unique and distinctive neighborhoods. When seen as a whole, Havana seems to have one character—an order probably attributed to the strong and persuasive Cuban culture. As times changed and the city evolved from a colonial provincial capital to a capital of an emerging new republic, it still maintained its holistic being, a unity of diverse parts. Havana's holistic image exists in contrast to the piecemeal development so often seen in twentieth-century cities, the result of ugly modernity, architecture that is either poorly designed or unsympathetic to its neighborhood, unimaginative planning, uninformed and an overzealous government and its bureaucracy, and the ever-aggressive encroachment of the automobile.

A City of Monuments

Havana is a noble city where monuments are an essential element expressing its culture and rich history while also acting as works of integral public art. Havana has many exemplary examples of monuments, both grand and modest. These monuments vary from pure sculpture such as the monument to the victims of the USS *Maine*, the statue of José Martí, and the monument to General Máximo Gómez, to the grand monuments of the dome of the capitol with its Statue of the Republic and edifices such as the Palacia Presidente.

In Havana, these monuments act as artistic focal points dispersed within the fabric of the city. They are arrows that point to and open up the vistas along Havana's grand boulevards. Two examples of such monuments are the two anchors to the promenade Paseo del Prado: the Capitolio and la Punta. The Paseo del Prado begins with the Capitolio in the south and continues to the fortress Castillo de San Salvador de la Punta on the Malecón in the north. Directly across the harbor entrance from la Punta, and originally connected by a large floating chain of wood and bronze rings, is Los Tres Reyes del Morro Castle. The silhouettes of the Morro Castle and the Malecón opening to the Straits of Florida have become the two important symbols of Havana.

At the foot of Paseo del Prado is a monument to the medical students executed by the Spanish on November 27, 1871, as punishment for their alleged desecration of the grave of a Spanish journalist. This marks the start of the Malecón, Havana's most important seaside boulevard. These monuments do not distract from their neighbors but rather complement the vistas and often set boundaries that define the city and its individual neighborhoods.

Havana has been a city that is both fun loving and spontaneous, but under this facade is a serious city—a city that captures its urban spaces and embraces them with historic and period buildings; speckles them with coffeehouses, street stalls, coffee stands, bars, and restaurants; then laces it all together with plazas, boulevards, esplanades, and a string of public gardens.

Monument to honor José Miguel Gómez, Avenida de los Presidentes, Vedado.

Monumento al General Máximo Gómez (1935), located on the north side of Avenida de los Estudiantes.
Sculptor: Aldo Gamba.

Top: This sculpture is part of the front of the Academia Naval de la Marina de Guerra building (Cuban Naval headquarters), located in Mariel near the Basilica Menor de San Francisco de Asís (1580–1591).

Above: Park and esplanade designed by Jean Claude Nicolas Forestier (1928) between Zulueta and Avenida de las Misiones, as seen from the Palacio Presidencial, looking to the Monumento al General Máximo Gómez and the Malecón.

Bas-relief at the base of the white marble Monumento al General Máximo Gómez (1935). Sculptor: Aldo Gamba.

It is a landscape of stone patios, iron streetlights, park benches, and lazy days, and a city of shaded colonnades and stately royal palms—all made electric with the dynamic movement of people. Havana is a city frozen in time and space, a city saturated with the hidden beat of Latin rhythms.

A City of Spaces

Havana is a city defined not by the individual buildings but by the spaces between. It is a city where mass is less significant than space. As Gordon Cullen states in the introduction to his seminal planning book *Townscape*, "the human being is constantly aware of his position in the environment, that he feels the need for a sense of place."[2]

To walk through Havana provides a sequence of revelations, of sudden contrasts bringing the city to life. As one walks through the streetscape, one senses the anticipation from the meandering streets or the feeling of enclosure from the defined spaces, all forms of the act of possession, which breathes life into the city. It is not a group of buildings but an opus.

Havana is a walking city of wide boulevards, defined by the parade of historic facades. Paseo del Prado is the most picturesque of Havana's tree-shaded walking streets, whose origin was Madrid's Paseo del Prado, the fashionable late-eighteenth-century strolling promenade built by Carlos III near Puerta de Alcala (City Gateway) and the urban fountain Plaza de Cibeles. However, Havana's Prado is probably more associated with Barcelona's las Ramblas (from the Arabic *rambla*, meaning "dried river bed"). Both are important pedestrian streets in their respective cities—centers for walking, meeting friends, or just enjoying the fresh air. They are promenades historically busy around the clock, particularly in the early evening hours, where Habaneros or Barcelonans traditionally would take their walks or, in earlier days, their carriage rides. Havana's promenade streets visually connect the city's various neighborhoods. It is this total interconnected social immersion, frozen in time at the turn of the twentieth century, that still makes Havana so wonderful and unique.

A City of Neighborhoods and Public Places

Havana's barrios (neighborhoods) are well defined, are relatively homogenous, and have a delightful domestic scale that permits, if one wishes, daily contact among neighbors. This concept of a pedestrian city as an environment for human contact has been largely lost in the contemporary car-dominated city, where the automobile has penetrated every crevice of the townscape. Each of Havana's main neighbor-

Havana, a city of public spaces alive with street commerce.

The Restaurante La Fuente del Patio, which opens to the Plaza de la Catedral, is part of the eighteenth-century Palacio de los Marquéses de Aguas Claras. This is an example of the pedestrian city, where human scale gives comfort and human contact flows within the city's neighborhood spaces.

hoods—Habana Vieja, Central Habana, Prado, El Vedado, and Miramar—is basically a reservoir of one architectural style created over one particular historic time, a relatively rare urban phenomenon. These distinct neighborhoods have an intelligible form that gives each its character and structure. Their lines of geographical demarcation are clear and obvious, whether it was the original city walls that defined Habana Vieja or the Rio Almendanes that divides El Vedado from the more elegant Miramar.

The streets of Havana used to be full of Habaneros—vendors (who have been harassed), busy walkers, strollers, and children playing. Each neighborhood today is flooded with the music of Latin rhythms being played on loud boom boxes for all to hear. The music not only bathes the streets but also effortlessly sweeps into every open window and the lives of those living within.

Havana is not a "park" or monumental city but a city of pedestrian-animated public spaces. It is an outdoor city of large plazas and small urban squares, historical monuments, and delightful sleepy public gardens graced with tall royal palms, and all defined by the surrounding classic and in most places human-scale buildings. The Spanish colonial streets of Habana Vieja mix beautifully with the turn-of-the-century rococo buildings built during the first breath of Cuban independence. In a city that has not been maintained for over fifty years, urban life hides among the ruins—ruins where the select few once lived in splendor and now where a multitude of small, human vignettes are played out each day in the crumbling mansions of Havana.

A Colonnaded City

The Romans created colonnaded cities that flowed seamlessly from one use to another, where the resultant shade and feeling of enclosure knitted the city together. A Roman citizen would awake in his or her atrium house, enjoy its colonnaded garden, and then proceed through the day basically shaded and protected. He or she would walk on mostly colonnaded streets to the marketplace, library, or temple and then to the theater, bath, or brothel. This system, so perfect for the tropics, was exported many centuries later to the Caribbean and to Havana, allowing the city to be both unified and continuous.

Edmund N. Bacon, the urban visionary, said that "the role of design in the city should be to create a harmonious environment for each individual who resides in it from the moment he rises in the morning until he retires at night . . . a movement system as a dominant organizing force in architectural design." He further writes on the design order of ancient Rome, "These were held together by the rhythm of the unifying post-and-lintel colonnades and similarly scaled rows of arches . . . brought

Top: Habaneros wait for the bus in the shade of a colonnade.

Above: Arcade, Palacio del Segundo Cabo, Plaza de Armas. The colonnades of the city provide shade and rain protection, weaving the city together.

Plaza Vieja with the musical and rhythmic shadows of its colonnades.

the scale down to one consonant with the rhythm of the rest of Rome's architecture."[3]

Central Habana is just such a colonnaded city, where Habaneros can walk in the shade when it's sunny and be dry while escaping a sudden tropical rain. They are always protected by the shaded arcade that takes on the architectural cloak of motherly comfort. Arcades surround Havana's plazas and were required by Havana's building code at the base of in-town buildings located on all principal avenues. This gave birth to the name of Alejo Carpentier's classic book, *La Ciudad de las Columnas*.

The rhythm of the arcades is repeated on Havana's traditional facade, where tall, thin windows and doors are common to articulate the building's design. Originally Havana's arcades were built to include the mezzanine floor: the slaves' and servants' floor sandwiched between the ground floor and the principal living floor above. When this mezzanine and its function were eliminated, the arcade was reduced in height, creating a more human-proportioned space both for the pedestrian using the arcade and for the building's facade, which then placed them more in scale with the pedestrian city.

A Mixed-Use City

Havana has become relatively unique in that it is still a mixed-use city. It challenges the illogic segregation of uses, the basis of zoning laws in most American cities. In this type of city, "small and scattered" has always been better than "regional and large." In many North American cities today, because of suburban sprawl and segregated zoning patterns, neighborhood shopping and services on a traditional "main street" are a thing of the past. However, in Havana, uses are mixed, and landmark buildings and cultural venues are scattered throughout the city's fabric so that each enriches a particular neighborhood. As an example, Habana Vieja has three public plazas or squares (described in chapter 2) and not the traditional single plaza. In Central Habana, there is still the traditional parade of small shops mixed with residential use that gives life to the streetscape.

In contrast to Havana, there is a new architectural style in America called "regional." Cities have taken up the call with regional malls, regional sports complexes, and regional performing arts centers. Everything in this type of automobile-driven society is regional. The regionalism of the American city requires giant collector roads that dissect the city and giant parking facilities that take huge portions of land, robbing the city of its continuity and creating a greater reliance on the automobile and the consumption of fossil fuel.

These arcaded and embellished buildings typify the marriage of fine architecture and the public spaces that they define, creating a total harmonious environment. Lower photo is of Casa de Dionisio Velasco (1912), designed by Francisco Ramírez Ovando.

In addition, regionalism, as opposed to the decentralized mixed-use facilities of Havana, robs individual neighborhoods of a stimulus for sustainability and healthy growth. The pedestrian and family neighborhood parade of little stores, which makes strolling and window-shopping such a delight, is now replaced with the agony and stress of driving and countless hours of lost time. One simple example of this new regional phenomenon in the automobile-dominated cities is the regional performing arts center. Here culture is packaged for suburban visits into or out of the city. Traditionally, the opera house, concert hall, or theater would be individual buildings enriching different neighborhoods. Obvious examples would be the Opera de Paris (Garnier, 1875), Milan's Teatro alla Scala (1778), Vienna's State Opera House (Staatsoper, 1869), and Barcelona's Palau de la Musica Catalana, a celebration of music, architecture, and applied art (1908). Regional performing arts centers are a new phenomenon in the United States, which started primarily with New York's Lincoln Center for the Performing Arts. Luckily, New York's Carnegie Hall (1890) was spared, and it still enriches its own neighborhood of the city.

A mixed-use city like Havana creates a swirling flow of urban life as a total, organic unity.

The juxtaposing of slum tenements in Central Havana with a Communist sign proclaiming "Here is Socialism." The tenements are in a state of obvious decay, set in the shadows, as is life in the slum. The walls are crumbling, and the paint vanished many years ago. The only thing clean and new in this photo is the sign proclaiming the glories of socialism.

Chapter 14

Defining a Common Purpose

Russian-style housing block, outskirts of Havana. This type of Soviet apartment block is always depressing and intrinsically ugly whether in Moscow, the former East Germany, or Havana. They were built during the period of Russian dominance, when the Kremlin sent experts to Cuba to teach and Cuba sent students to Russia to learn. Architecture was obviously not one of the Russians' strong subjects. These buildings are built as unadorned hunks deliberately elongated with a series of individual entrances to each apartment column in order that there would be no public lobbies or spaces where groups might gather and become a problem for the state.

A City of Neglect

Although the basic urban footprint of the city has not been destroyed, present-day Havana is a city of neglect and decay. Cities and societies over time are either infused with the spirit of continual renewal and regeneration or are permitted to fall into a state of atrophy and decay, as is the case of Havana today. The superstructure of the city in general is in a condition of architectural decomposition. New construction, restoration, and routine maintenance during the last half a century have been almost nonexistent except for the huge, oppressive, Russian-style apartment structures built on the city's outskirts during the Russian era; some hotels built by European entrepreneurs; and the very visible, tourist-motivated reconstruction on the preplanned walking streets of Habana Vieja. Here the new ruling elite plan the visitor's visit through a series of vignettes of restored historic buildings and promenades that present a false facade of a city otherwise in terrible decay.

Havana today is like a once-beautiful movie starlet of a past era, now forgotten and faded, an old woman in her storied but decaying mansion, with clothes old and out of fashion, her face deeply wrinkled, unable to hide her age with layers of thick makeup, her past reflected only in a faded twinkle in her eyes.

Havana's neighborhoods are still the same, unlike most contemporary cities that have been destroyed by the brutal and inconsiderate modern architecture of the last half of the twentieth century, suburban sprawl, oppressive traffic, and ever-consuming roadways and expressways. Castro's policies have inadvertently preserved the underlining urban pattern of the city.

The totalitarianism imposed upon the Cuban people has put the city into a deep sleep, a hypnotic trance, from which—someday—it will awake. The government that controls all has not been able to maintain or restore the vast majority of the city.

Buildings in the tropics, in environments such as Havana, deteriorate at a rapid pace, particularly without continuous and proper maintenance. The bright and harsh sun and its ultraviolet rays quickly destroy paint and other protective coatings. Heavy tropical rains bring moisture, leaks, mildew, and fungi. Thin cracks in the concrete, once penetrated, soon corrode the concrete's steel reinforcing, causing it to rust, swell, and then spalling the concrete. In the tropics, wood rots quickly, insects and rodents are plentiful, vegetation is aggressive, and hurricanes and storms

Top: Most of Havana is in a state of decomposition, with no maintenance or repairs having been undertaken for half a century. The only restoration has occurred in areas carefully chosen by the government as avenues of "showcase" buildings, which give the false impression of a city in the bloom of health. This photo shows a touch of humor with the interplay of persons living in close proximity in this high-density city.

Above: Arcade on the Malecón, near the intersection with the Paseo del Prado, traditionally a prime and important location in Havana. This is part of what was originally a stately row of arcaded buildings now in a sad state of decay. The once gay and tropical luminous pastel colors are now just hints of their former glory.

This classic entry arch in Habana Vieja shows the state of disintegration of most of Havana. Here the walls present impressionistic compositions of faded and peeling paint with no trace of maintenance. The transom is broken, allowing the elements to enter and further damage the interior spaces. The faces of resignation are clear on those who use this portal for a little shade and rest.

Left: Calle Reina Central Habana. Originally this kitchen was part of an important, grand mansion in Havana. The large hood testifies to the opulent lifestyle of the wealthy aristocratic class in earlier times. Imagine the huge roasts prepared by the household slaves for a formal dinner. Now this kitchen shelters an entire family, where they cook on the small stove. The nearby buckets collect water from the leaking ceiling.

Below: A bedroom in Habana Vieja. Several families now live in a home originally built for one family. The makeshift bed is supported on concrete blocks and heavy timbers, the walls are tattered with peeling paint, yet the occupants keep what they have neat and tidy. The decay is not because the occupants don't want to repair their home, but because they cannot. The bedpan under the bed is a potent symbol, speaking volumes about the state of the city's infrastructure.

In a tenement in Central Habana, this compartmented
toilet is the only sanitary facility that many families share.
There is little privacy, for it opens to a common walk and a
shared court. Its state of cleanliness, sanitation, and maintenance is obvious. This is the part of Havana that most
tourists never see.

A central court in a typical Havana tenement and slum. Here many families—too many—
live in squalor, crowded into little space, while sharing the only source of light and air, the
laundry-filled court.

are numerous. Add to all this outdated and exposed electrical and plumbing systems and the continuous fifty years of decomposing chaos.

Theodore Dalrymple, in "Why Havana Had to Die," from his book *Our Culture, What's Left of It*, relates to Havana's ruination:

> The splendor is very faded. . . . The stucco has given way to mold; roofs have gone, replaced by corrugated iron; shutters have crumbled into sawdust; paint is a phenomenon of the past; staircases end in precipices; windows lack glass; doors are off their hinges; interior walls have collapsed; wooden props support, though not with any degree of assurance, all kinds of structures; ancient electrical wiring emerges from walls like worms from cheese; wrought ironwork balconies crumble into rust; plaster peels as in a malignant skin disease. . . . Every grand and beautifully proportioned room . . . has been subdivided by plywood partitions into smaller spaces, in which entire families now live. . . . No ruination is too great to render a building unfit for habitation.[1]

The normal, organic growth of a city requires freedom, freedom to create and freedom to compete, for monopoly in any form breeds stagnation and a listless society. The Communist government controls every aspect of Havana's urban life, and its bureaucracy has imposed a rigid system of conformity, controlling property rights, ownership, and construction methods. The totality of this rigid control discourages proper maintenance so necessary, particularly in the tropical seafront environment. This massive urban neglect for fifty years is the consequence of a totalitarian system that has stifled self-expression, creativity, and the competitive spirit necessary to refurbish and sustain a city. This has resulted in Havana being in a state of decomposition. To quote from Jaime Suchlicki's book *Columbus to Castro and Beyond*: "A highly intolerant and hierarchical party structure has developed. It has been molded through the successful attempts of the leadership to monopolize political functions such as recruitment, socialization, and articulation, as well as to inculcate uniformity of beliefs and conformity of behavior within the party and throughout society."[2]

Dalrymple observes about Havana and the car: "And the comparative lack of traffic in Havana demonstrates how mixed a blessing the inexorable spread of the automobile has been for the quality of city life. Had Havana developed 'normally,' its narrow grid-pattern streets would by now be choking with traffic and pollution, a suffocating inferno like Guatemala City or San Jose, Costa Rica, where to breathe is to grow breathless, where noise makes the ears sing, and where thoughts turn to escape as soon as possible."[3]

Public transportation is an essential ingredient in a pedestrian-based city. Long lines of people wait far from the bus stop, and people are called to the bus one at a time by a government official so that tourists do not see the large number of people waiting.

An Organic, Pedestrian City

Freed from the automobile, Havana has open colonnades, public plazas, waterfront promenades, and tree-shaded boulevards where the pedestrian has been given dignity. These pedestrian-friendly environments serve as outdoor rooms that lace together the fabric of Havana. These pedestrian enclaves act as eddies lessening the intensity of modern city life. They give Habaneros an aura of comfort, protection, and the feeling of being master of "their home town."

Havana is a walking city. Walking the Malecón along the Caribbean Sea and tasting its fresh salt air, especially at sunset, is special. Walking through the Old City is a walk through a history book of a time gone by. Walking along the tree-lined Paseo del Prado is to enjoy children at play and neighbors in leisurely conversation. Walking through some parts of El Vedado or Miramar is an immersion in the idealized "City Beautiful."

The late Jane Jacobs, acknowledged as one of the great thinkers in the twentieth century on the art of city, wrote, "The simple needs of automobiles are more easily understood and satisfied than the complex needs of cities, and a growing number of planners and designers have come to believe that if they can only solve the problems of traffic, they will thereby have solved the major problem of cities."[4]

Havana has been literally saved by the absence of the automobile during the isolating dictatorship of Fidel Castro. Since the government has prohibited the sale of new automobiles to the population, the unforeseen consequence is that the city's pedestrian fabric has been preserved. Hopefully, in the post–Fidel Castro era of reconstruction, the traffic engineers will not destroy this proud city. The form of Havana is still an organic, holistic city animated by a few well-kept 1950s two-tone Chevrolets, kinetic sculptures, and relics of a bygone era.

Havana is obviously not the answer to all global urban problems, but within it are the seeds to solving some of these problems. It has part of the answer. Havana has the classic order, neighborhood balance, architectural elegance, and pedestrian harmony that urban planners have longed for.

"Cities are an immense laboratory of trial and error, failure and success, in city building and city design. This is the laboratory in which city planning should have been learning and forming and testing its theories," wrote Jane Jacobs.[5] Havana, one of the world's great hidden cities, is a city whose character must be understand and preserved in Cuba's inevitable period of transition from Communist dictatorship to freedom, a time that will surely come.

This book is dedicated to the understanding of Havana's urban presence and its special architecture. This work hopefully can in some small way reinforce the historic concept of a city as a work of cultural art. This idea can be revisited as cities

Good public transportation is an essential ingredient in any restoration and rebuilding of Havana. The humpbacked *camello* truck-drawn trailer-bus pictured here has been the bane of Havana's commuters. The *camellos* are currently being replaced by more comfortable Chinese buses, yet with less passenger capacity and no air-conditioning.

The automobile, the enabler that destroys.

understand their potential of becoming places of human scale and noble neighborhoods where social dreams come true. Havana, once restored, could serve as an example for other cities to change from being strictly utilitarian bastions of apathy into holistic cities of beauty. Havana can serve as an example for others, while in return its lessons, once understood, could aid in Havana's own preservation.

Havana historically is a city whose buildings do not shout for individual attention, but rather blend harmoniously into the total urban fabric in a simple, dignified way. The Spanish colonial streets of Habana Vieja mix beautifully with the turn-of-the-century rococo buildings built during the first breath of Cuban independence.

Simply stated, Havana is an innately beautiful city with a large depository of historic styles, basically preserved and concentrated in relatively defined, homogenous neighborhoods. These neighborhoods, once restored, will form a treasure house of historic periods and styles.

All this is true, despite the fact that the face of Havana is now in a deteriorated state of disrepair after fifty years of isolation and total neglect. However, the sound underlying structure of Havana still bleeds through its peeling walls and fractured facades, waiting to be restored and renewed. Havana is a giant laboratory ready to be unlocked.

The colors of Havana are faded today with a patina of old age, yet they still seem strangely bright in the tropical sun. There is the sparkling white spray of the salt-scented Caribbean Sea as it crashes against the gray walls of the famous promenade, the Malecón. Here young boys fish and lovers still stroll, silhouetted against the background of pastel-colored arcades, crumbling and unpainted since the revolution. Havana's stone fortress built of stone cut out of the coastal reef still symbolically protects the harbor and shines with the golden glow of the late afternoon Caribbean light.

This tropical rainbow recalls the days when Havana was the jewel of the Spanish colonial crown, a memory that is reinforced when one walks through the seventeenth- and eighteenth-century streets of Habana Vieja, streets that weave around the once-proud colonial buildings. One must think of Havana not as a collection of buildings, albeit some outstanding buildings, but rather as an entity complete unto itself—a total city modeled by its strong historic past and directed by a culture and people that are creative, dynamic, and culturally unique.

Celebrity Architecture

Havana is unique among the great cities of the world, for due to its harsh, rigid, government-controlled property system, it has been spared the fashionable trend of celebrity: ego architecture. In our contemporary world fanned by television and the print media, the celebrity is honored and even revered. We have celebrity athletes, celebrity entertainers, and now celebrity architects who create celebrity buildings for cities that starve to be celebrity cities; it is called ego architecture. It is architecture designed by elitist architects in an obscene scramble for individual glory with no concern for the context of the city.

This self-centered architecture started in the 1920s as a socialist ideal born to create workers' housing by European architects in academia and was called the International Style; Walter Gropius, Ludwig Mies van der Rohe, Le Corbusier, and other architectural intellectuals were its leaders. It looked down on centuries of historic and traditional architecture as bourgeoisie. Their manifestos called houses "machines for living" and allowed only plain surfaces, flat roofs, the color white, and exposed concrete structures. In his brilliant book *From Bauhaus to Our House*, Tom Wolfe portrays the lack of architectural options in modern architecture by describing Mies van der Rohe's glass boxes on the campus of the Illinois Institute of Technology: "The main classroom building looked like a shoe factory. The chapel looked like a power plant."[6] Architecture was reduced to a repetitive, elitist style where all choices were the same. These superstars were the "anointed ones," and their style spread throughout the world to places as remote as the new residential neighborhoods of 1930s Havana, fortunately in only small doses. Today the concept of celebrity architecture has gone from minimal to maximum, from the box to flamboyant sculpture, but it is still cold, stark, white, and blind to the traditions of local culture. Havana luckily is one of the few cities spared, so far, from the fate of celebrity architecture.

When we worship anything as an object, whether a person or a building, we often lose sight of the totality and inherent unity that people and objects should have with their surroundings. If we had to choose in a city between visual chaos with an occasional great building or harmony, order, and unity without greatness, we would choose the latter. Havana is an example of a harmonious city that does not worship architecture but embraces it. Its important buildings do not dominate but blend and define its spaces. Havana is a narrative, unfolding over time. Its story seems to never end, and its future is still to be written. Even when a city does not seem to change in fifty years, it changes anyway because of its climate of neglect and the depreciation it endures. The cult of celebrity has become a religion, or at least an elitist pastime. Havana so far has been spared the curse of ego architecture.

Restoring the City

The architecture of Havana is the fossil remains of centuries of Cuban culture. This past is defined by the city's architecture, boulevards, and public plazas. The restoration of Havana will require close cooperation between the government and the private sector to maintain this cultural quality while incorporating modern conveniences and technology. Cuba's new society will have to prepare and implement plans at the national, regional, and local levels to deal with the requirements of a new social order.

In the case of Havana, two types of early actions will have to be initiated. First, there is the need for the reconstruction of water and sewage systems, together with transportation and communication services, while renovating and updating housing inventories. Second, the tourist infrastructure must be developed, considering a series of integrated demands, each one with unique characteristics, such as the construction of cruise ship terminals and support systems and the enhancement of the environmental conditions of Havana Bay by improving the water quality through the elimination of major sources of pollution. It is extremely important that the development of well-designed tropical and human-scale hotels and restaurants be closely regulated. This will allow for optimal site utilization and limit the environmental impact on the city's historical and cultural characteristics while implementing a street code for minimizing obtrusive signage. In addition, creating a comprehensive shade tree ordinance will preserve, enlarge, and enhance Havana's existing tree canopy.

These and other actions will provide the context of complex and expensive plans for the redevelopment of Cuba, but it is evident that Havana is an important Cuban resource. The challenge for a democratic Cuba is to deal with the present-day problems of urban degradation, rebuilding its public works and services, refurbishing its electric grid, improving its water and sewer systems and public transportation, while at the same time saving the historical and cultural values.

Havana, under its veil of almost total decay, has traditionally been fundamentally a city for all the senses: a city of vision, light, volume, texture, decoration, symbolism, rhythm, space, touch, sound, smell, taste, movement, dance, and the celebration of the Cuban way of life.

Havana is a city whose basic neighborhood patterns are in suspended animation, frozen in time and space. Nonetheless, since the 1960s Havana has become a city in almost total decay. The government that controls all has not been able to initiate the desire to maintain or restore the vast majority of the city. This is due in large part to the shunting of construction material to huge nonproductive military projects (tunnels) and gigantic nonpractical civilian endeavors.

Palacio del Centro Gallego—The silhouettes of Havana are expressed in a myriad of ways.

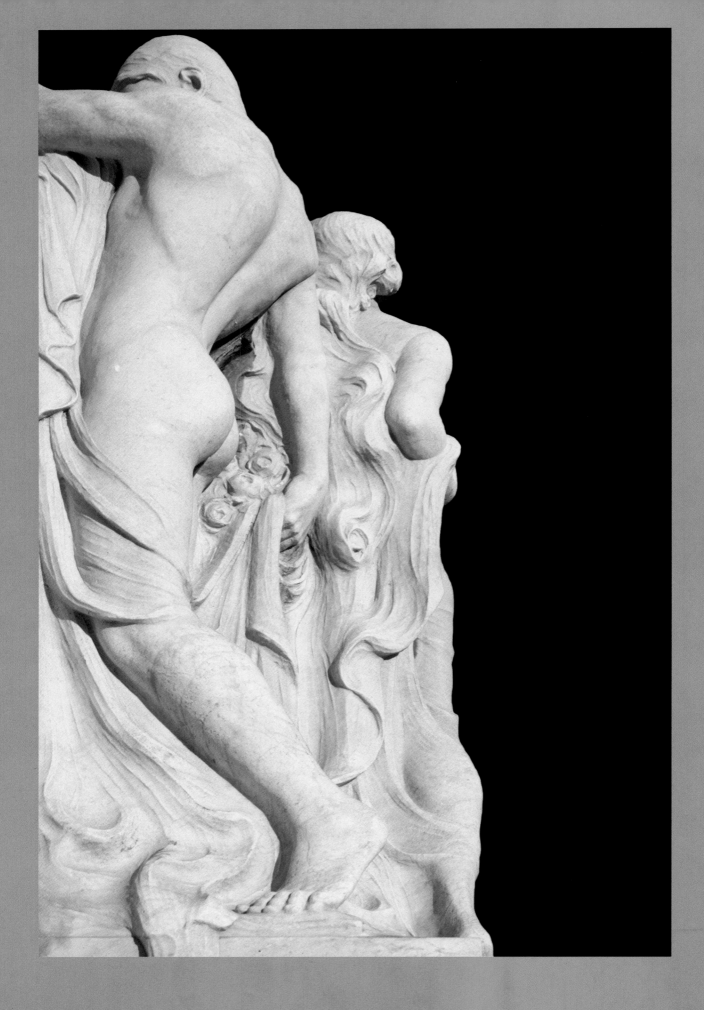

The normal organic growth of a city requires freedom—freedom to create, freedom to compete—for monopoly in any form breeds stagnation and a listless society. Havana is a city crushed by a harsh, totalitarian dictatorship, oppressed without the opportunity of dissent, without freedom. The Communist government controls every aspect of Havana's urban life. Its bureaucracy has imposed a rigid system of conformity, controlling property rights, ownership, and construction methods. The totality of this rigid control discourages proper maintenance so necessary in the tropical, seafront environment.

Architectural Principles for Sensitive Growth

Let us think about a future roadmap of managed, controlled, and sensitive growth where an enlightened citizenship, caring architects, developers, and historic preservationists work together to maintain Havana's rich cultural, urban, and architectural heritage.

The guiding concepts to sustain Havana's unique urban presence could include the following principles: the preservation of its gardens, plazas, boulevards, and arcades, all suited for the pedestrian and the need for shade, harmony, and beauty; respect for Havana's tropical climate and native vegetation; the maintenance of its urban organization with its defined, individualistic, and homogeneous neighborhoods with their unifying codes, circulation, and dimensions; the importance of shade trees and their canopy, which soften the city's palette and bathe the city in a soft light; the continuation of the city's Spanish heritage of public spaces, plazas, and parks, where the spaces are often more important than the buildings that surround them; the discouraging of urban sprawl and the encouragement of well-designed, high-density, mixed-use neighborhoods of townhouses, terrace houses, and midrise apartments, where people live within a walk or bike ride from where they work, shop, and recreate; the continuation of the existing street topography, which encourages the free flow of people in a human-scale and pedestrian comfortable environment.

Cities Are Frail

Cities, always seemingly timeless, built of eternal concrete and steel, are thought, at the time of creation, to be immortal. In reality, they are frail, very frail. Havana is always threatened, under the ravages of old age, political oppression, the souring tropical sun, the mist of corrosive sea air, cyclical hurricanes and tropical storms, and, worst of all, the force of people as they neglect, remodel, remake, renovate, rebuild, and replan, often without understanding or remorse.

Unsympathetic and unbridled real-estate development unleashed by a tidal wave of free-market forces can—in a few years of modernity—destroy and overpower Havana's half a millennium of historic, organic growth with massive, out-of-scale and out-of-character modern construction. Havana's preservation and revival depend on the appreciation of its extraordinary quality as a fabled city. This book is written not to predict Havana's future but to try, in a small way, to influence it at its moment of awakening.

Havana is the reflection in stone of the unique and pulsating Cuban culture. Havana embraces both a reality and a dream—the realization of its turbulent past and the eternal promise for its future. Havana is a song sung to blaring trumpets, a dance danced to wild Afro-Cuban bongos, roasted pork, and strong, aged rum. Havana's spirit, its animated principles of life, and its substance, as well as its architectural presence, are one. Here there is no division between spirit and matter, the sacred and the secular. Havana can be a symphony where the spirit of the Cuban culture and people are united, where physical and spiritual harmony are one.

Dream a dream. Plant a garden. Help it grow.

Epilogue

The Doomsday Scenario

An Art Deco high-rise, the Lopez Serrano Building (1932).
Architects: Ricardo Mira and Miguel Rosich.

ON ONE LONG-AWAITED MORNING, the light of freedom will shine brightly on the Bay of Havana, and Cuba will be free once again.

Of the many scenarios concerning the urban future of Havana, we should discuss three possibilities. The first two envision a time when freedom comes relatively quickly to this wonderful island, and Havana is either restored with dignity and restraint or caught in a frenzy of an urban freefall. The third prospect—and the most likely—will be a gradual and evolutionary political change that will affect the city in gradual and subtle ways. The picture of this is skillfully drawn in the afterword by Jaime Suchlicki, the eminent Cuban scholar at the University of Miami. Now let us discuss the two possibilities for Havana's urban future that would happen in a relatively quick return to freedom.

In one, Havana, even after the staggering amount of money needed to restore the city, experiences a slow and healthy restoration with an enlightened citizenship, proper zoning codes, and an honest government to enforce them. This is what this book is all about and the future we all hope for.

The other darker and most disturbing possibility—presented here for its shock effect and what the true lovers of Havana would detest—is what could be called "The Doomsday Scenario," and it could go something like this.

When Cuba is opened to U.S. travel and investment, there will be a feeding frenzy among eager, pent-up Americans. On that very hour, the cruise ships that flood the Caribbean will change destinations and start heading for the docks of Havana. These giant-size super cruise ships, with their thousands of passengers, will be stacked up ten abreast. Throngs of eager passengers will pour ashore with cameras and guidebooks in hand. The tour buses will be lined up in an endless caravan with guides holding high-numbered signs and small, brightly colored flags flying in endless rows. Oh, what a sight to chill the soul!

Souvenir shops will line both sides of Obispo Street, obliterating any of the "old and quaint" architecture that may still be behind. But it won't matter, because the tour books and postcards will have better pictures than any point-and-shoot digital camera can take. The Web will be clogged with photos and videos, and everybody will publish a book on their adventure. The T-shirt shops will be everywhere, even exceeding those that now line Duval Street in once "picturesque" old Key West.

Then, after this first wave, the invasion will continue with the arrival of the hotel developers. Every hotel chain in the world, big or small, expensive or cheap, will scurry for the best sites. There will be no zoning or political control when the money starts to flow. The race will be on to build the biggest, the greatest, the newest, the glitziest, the tallest hotel that money can be borrowed to build. Restaurants will follow in a third wave—Italian, French, Chinese, Californian, and Mexican, every theme and in every color, even "Caribbean cuisine" for that "local" flavor. The bills will be expensive, the food will be slow or fast, the chains everywhere, with only a few independents scattered between. The job market will boom, and the money will flow.

With that infusion of money, a wave of new automobiles will surely follow. The new dealerships will sell the latest models, while the Habana Vieja 1950s Chevys will be sold to collectors who will arrive like miners to the Klondike for the gold rush. The new cars will quickly be followed by expressways, express lanes, overpasses, underpasses, clover leafs, and parking garages—all engineered to destroy the neighborhoods and the pedestrian city while making driving easier and safer until the next construction project starts widening the roads in an endless cycle of exhaust, delays, and frustration.

The next assault will come from the condominium developers who, having run out of land or luck in the United States, will flock to a fresh "field" to plunder. Cranes will be everywhere, probably sent over from Shanghai or Miami. These developers will buy whatever old houses or lots are left over from the hotel developers. The computer-designed condos will be big and tall, with masts and towers on top and with distinctive curves, glamorous lobbies, and endless pools, offering units with limited peeks of the bay while most will gaze on the broad vistas of the condos next door and down the street. The condos will blanket Havana's historic skyline. A skyline can be picturesque with a few domes or towers, but the distinctive skyline will disappear with this dense, high-rise forest, where every tree fights for light to grow and air to breathe. What a place to sell condos and timeshares—the tropics, the weather, the excitement, and you are part of the latest "new adventure" in the world! The harbor, full of yachts, will compete with the new Havana International Airport as the biggest and the best.

To fan the flames even brighter, the advertising and public relations firms, the models, the fashion designers, and the celebrities will want to find their place in the mambo sun. The beautiful mansions will be spruced up, and the Old City will become a continuous movie set with television cameras, and not far behind will be *Habana Vice*, *Habana PD*, and *CSI Habana*. Imagine the sun setting over the Malecón while the latest Ferrari races alone down its winding path. Could anyone resist?

Oh, the splendor of it all!

Afterword

An Uncertain Future

JAIME SUCHLICKI

In this beautiful and sophisticated book, Kenneth Treister, Felipe Préstamo, and Raul Garcia discuss two possibilities for the future of Havana. One, a bright future with slow, orderly growth, or a second one: fast, chaotic, and less desirable, propelled by a "feeding frenzy among eager, pent-up Americans." Under this latter scenario, Havana would transform into more of a tourist destination with a lopsided U.S. tourist-oriented economy.

Yet there may be a third, more ominous future for the once-beautiful capital memorialized in this book and in Andy Garcia's film *The Lost City*. Under the leadership of a government unwilling to provide major changes, both internally and in its relations with the United States, Havana would continue to deteriorate and flounder. It is likely that Raul Castro and his immediate successors will try to cling to power without moving Cuba to a market economy and without providing meaningful concessions to the United States that could lead to a normalization of relations.

General Raul Castro's regime faces significant challenges. A bankrupt economy, popular unhappiness, the need to maintain order and discipline in the population at large, and the need to increase productivity within the labor force are some of the more pressing problems. Raul Castro is critically dependent on the military. Lacking the charisma and legitimacy of his brother, he also needs the support of key party leaders and technocrats within the government bureaucracy. He is therefore creating a framework for collective leadership controlled by the military. Since assuming power, he has introduced a series of economic adjustments. It is probable that after a period of consolidation and harsh repressive rule, this leadership will initiate limited economic reforms but not political changes.

Perhaps the critical challenge for the Raul Castro regime is to balance the need to improve the economy and satisfy the needs of the population while maintaining continuous political control. Too rapid economic reforms may lead to a loosening of political control, a fact feared by Raul Castro, the military, and other allies bent on remaining in power. Some overtures to the United States also seem possible after a period of time, especially if no major opposition develops within the island. While maintaining an anti–United States posture, a consolidated Raul Castro regime may welcome American tourists and limited U.S. trade and investments.

Under this slow and most likely succession scenario, limited political and economic changes would take place. While a significant number of U.S. citizens would visit Cuba if the U.S. travel ban were to be lifted, investment would be on a small scale. If the U.S. embargo were modified or lifted, trade would develop as U.S. companies attempt to penetrate the Cuban market and stake a claim, as some Canadian and European companies have already done.

Given Cuba's need for all types of products and consumer goods, the potential for trade is significant. Yet demand alone is not sufficient. Cuba must have the ability to pay for foreign goods and services. These resources will come initially from tourist dollars spent on the island. Eventually, Cuba must sell its products—primarily tobacco, agriculture, seafood, oil, and nickel—in the U.S. market.

Investments would be limited, however, given the lack of an extensive internal market, the uncertainties surrounding the long-term risk to foreign investment, an uncertain political situation, and the opportunities provided by other markets in Latin America and elsewhere. Modest initial investments would be directed primarily to exploiting Cuba's tourist, mining, and natural resources industries.

Unless major reforms take place, it is unlikely that the U.S. government or corporations will be willing to commit significant investment funds in Cuba. The U.S. government could provide limited financial aid but would not grant Cuba other benefits such as Caribbean Basin Initiative (CBI) or North American Free Trade Agreement (NAFTA) membership. Foreign investments would be limited in scope as U.S. firms wait for Cuban measures that would assure investors that the reforms taking place are irreversible and that they represent a major step toward a comprehensive transformation of the economy.

Under this slow transition scenario, any post–Raul Castro government will face significant challenges and problems. There will be the awesome task of economic reconstruction. Cuba's extreme dependence on Soviet bloc trade and the adaptation of its economy to an unnatural and immense subsidy inflow for nearly four decades created an artificial economy, which disappeared and has been partially replaced by dependence on Venezuela and China. Cuba does not have a viable economy of its own. As nearly every category of imports keeps decreasing, a vicious circle of poverty descends without mercy.

Cuba has a weak internal market. Consumption is limited by a strict and severe rationing system. Whatever transactions take place outside this system are in the black market, which operates with dollars and merchandise stolen from state enterprises or received from abroad. The Cuban peso has depreciated considerably, and its purchasing power has decreased. Huge and persistent government deficits and the absence of virtually any stabilizing fiscal and monetary policies have accelerated the downward spiraling of the economy.

Production of sugar, Cuba's mainstay export, has dropped to levels comparable to those of the Great Depression era, and prices of other Cuban commodities continue their downward trend in international markets.

In addition to these vexing economic realities, there will be also a maze of legal problems posed by the issue of the legality of foreign investments and the validity of property rights acquired during the Fidel Castro era. Obviously, Cuban nationals, Cuban Americans, and foreigners whose properties were confiscated during the early years of the revolution will want to reclaim them or will ask for fair compensation as soon as this becomes feasible. The United States and other countries whose citizens' assets were seized without compensation stand ready to support their nationals' claims. Cubans living abroad await the opportunity to exercise their legal claims before Cuban courts. The Eastern European and Nicaraguan examples are good indications of the complexities, delays, and uncertainties accompanying the reclamation process.

Cuba's severely damaged infrastructure is also in need of major rebuilding. The outdated electric grid cannot supply the meager needs of consumers and industry; transportation services are totally insufficient; communication facilities are obsolete; and sanitary and medical facilities have deteriorated so badly that contagious diseases of epidemic proportions constitute a real menace to the population. In addition, environmental concerns such as pollution of bays and rivers are in need of immediate attention.

Economic and legal problems are not, however, the only challenges facing Cuba's future. One of the critical problems is the continuous power of the military. In the past, Cuba had a strong tradition of militarism. During recent years, the military, as an institution, has acquired unprecedented power. Under any conceivable scenario, the military will continue to be a key, decisive player. Not unlike Nicaragua, Cuba may develop a limited democratic system with Cubans able to elect civilian leaders but with the military exercising real power and remaining the final arbiter of the political process.

Any immediate significant reduction of the military may be difficult, if not impossible. A powerful and proud institution, the armed forces would see any attempt to undermine their authority as an unacceptable intrusion into their affairs and as a threat to their existence. The military's control of key economic sectors under the Castro regime will make it more difficult in the future to dislodge the military from these activities and to limit its role to a strictly military one. Reducing the size of the armed forces will be problematic as the economy may not be able to absorb the unemployed members of the military or the government may not be able to retrain military personnel fast enough to occupy civilian positions.

The role of the military will also be determined in part by social conflicts that may emerge. For the first half a century of the Cuban republic, political violence was an important factor in society—a belief developed in the legitimacy of violence to effect political changes. Such violence will probably reemerge with a vengeance in the future. The Castro Communist rule has engendered profound hatred and resentments. Political vendettas will be rampant; differences over how to restructure society will be profound; factionalism in society and in the political process will be common. It will be difficult to create mass political parties as numerous leaders and groups vie for power and develop ideas on how to organize society, what to do about the economy, what type of regime should be established, and how to unravel the legacy of decades of Communist dictatorship.

A free and restless labor movement will complicate matters for any future government. During the Fidel Castro era, the labor movement remained docile and under continuous government control. Only one unified, Castro-controlled labor movement has been allowed. In a democratic Cuba, labor will not be a passive instrument of any government. Rival labor organizations will develop programs for labor vindication and demand better salaries and welfare for their members. A militant, vociferous, and difficult-to-manage labor movement will surely characterize Cuba's future.

Similarly, the apparent harmonious race relations of the Castro era may collapse in a free society. There has been a gradual Africanization of the Cuban population over the past several decades. In part because of greater intermarriage and miscegenation, in part because of the out-migration of more than a million mostly white Cubans, there is a greater proportion of blacks and mulattoes in Cuba. This has led to some fear and resentment among whites on the island. On the other hand, blacks believe that they have been left out of the political process, as whites still dominate the higher echelons of the government's power structure. The dollarization of the economy has accentuated these differences, with blacks receiving fewer dollars from abroad. The potential exists for significant racial tension, as these feelings and frustrations are aired in a democratic and free environment.

One of the most difficult problems that Cuba faces is that of acceptance of, and obedience to, the law. Every day Cubans violate Communist laws: they steal from state enterprises; they participate in the black market; they engage in all types of illegal activities, including widespread graft and corruption. They do this to survive. Eradication of those necessary vices from the past will not be easy in the future, especially since many of these predate the Castro era. Graft and corruption, as well as disobedience of laws, have been endemic in Cuba since colonial times. "Obedezco pero no cumplo" (I will implement the laws but not obey them) is one of the most lasting and pervasive Spanish legacies to Cuba and the Latin American world.

The unwillingness of the Cubans to obey laws will be matched by their unwillingness to sacrifice and endure the difficult years that will follow the end of Communism. An entire generation has grown up under the constant exhortations and pressures of the Communist leadership to work hard and sacrifice more for society. The young, particularly those who grew up since the collapse of the Soviet Union, are alienated from the political process and are eager for a better life. Many want to migrate to the United States. If the present rate of requests for visas at the U.S. consular office in Havana is any indication, more than two million Cubans want to move permanently to the United States. Under a U.S.-Cuban normalization of relations, Cubans will be free to visit the United States. Many will come as tourists and stay as illegal immigrants. Others will be claimed as legal immigrants by their relatives who are already naturalized citizens of the United States. A significant out-migration from Cuba is certain, posing an added major problem for U.S. immigration authorities in particular and for U.S. policy in general at a time of increasing anti-immigration feelings and legislation in the United States.

While many Cubans will want to leave Cuba, few Cuban Americans would abandon their life in the United States and return to the island, especially if Cuba experiences a slow and painful transition period. Although those exiles who are allowed to return will be welcomed initially as business partners and investors, they will be resented, especially as they become involved in domestic politics. Adjusting the views and values of the exile population to those of the island will be a difficult and lengthy process.

The future of Cuba is therefore clouded with problems and uncertainties. More than five decades of Communism will surely leave profound scars on Cuban society. As in Eastern Europe and Nicaragua, reconstruction may be slow, painful, and not totally successful. Unlike these countries, Cuba has at least three unique advantages: proximity to, and a long tradition of close relations with, the United States; a major tourist attractiveness; and a large and wealthy exile population. These three factors could converge to transform Cuba's economy, but only if the Cuban leadership creates the necessary conditions: an open, legally fair economy and an open, tolerant, and responsible political system. Unfortunately, life in Cuba is likely to remain difficult and improve slowly, and Havana will continue to suffer.

Jaime Suchlicki is the Emilio Bacardi Moreau Distinguished Professor and Director, Institute for Cuban and Cuban-American Studies, University of Miami. He is the author of *Cuba: From Columbus to Castro and Beyond*, now in its fifth edition.

Notes

Preface

1. Gordon Cullen, *Townscape* (New York: Reinhold, 1961), 7.
2. Lewis Mumford, *The City in History: Its Origins, Its Transformations, and Its Prospects* (New York: Harcourt, Brace and World, 1961), 402.

Prologue

1. Kirkpatrick Sale, *The Conquest of Paradise: Christopher Columbus and the Columbian Legacy* (New York: Random House, 1990), 38.
2. George Mitchell, ed., *Architecture of the Islamic World: Its History and Social Meaning* (London: Thames and Hudson, 1978), 7.

Chapter 1. From Village to Walled City (1519–1762)

1. Irene A. Wright, *Historia documental de San Cristobal de La Habana en el siglo XVI*, 2 vols. (Havana: Academia de la Historia de Cuba, 1927), 49.
2. Joaquin Weiss, *La arquitectura colonial cubana. Siglos XVI al XIX* (Havana: Instituto Cubano del Libro, and Seville: Juanta de Andalucía, 1996), 160.
3. Juliet Barclay, *Havana: Portrait of a City* (London: Cassell, 1993), 60.

Chapter 2. Growth and Change in the Walled City

1. Barclay, *Havana*, 107.
2. Martha De Castro y de Cardelas, *El arte en Cuba* (Miami: Edicones Universal, 1940), 330.
3. Weiss, *Arquitectura colonial cubana*, 275.
4. Robert Hughes, *Barcelona* (New York: Alfred A. Knopf, 1992), 271.
5. Weiss, *Arquitectura colonial cubana*, 267.
6. Barclay, *Havana*, 64.
7. Sidney David Markman, *Colonial Architecture of Antiqua Guatemala* (Philadelphia: American Philosophical Society, 1966), 87.

Chapter 3. From Walled Colonial City to the Capital of the Republic

1. Joseph L. Scarpaci, Roberto Segre, and Mario Coyula, *Havana: Two Faces of the Antillean Metropolis* (Chapel Hill: University of North Carolina Press, 2002), 47.
2. Barclay, *Havana*, 159.
3. Ibid., 179.
4. Ibid., 181.
5. Scarpaci, Segre, and Coyula, *Havana*, 28.
6. http://www.ideco.com/fans.

Chapter 4. Havana at the Turn of the Twentieth Century

1. Scarpaci, Segre, and Coyula, *Havana*, 14, 34.
2. Francesco Abbate, *Art Nouveau: The Style of the 1890s* (New York: Octopus Books, 1972), chapter 1.

Chapter 5. Spanish Colonial Architecture

1. Mitchell, *Architecture*, 10–11.
2. Ibid., 13.
3. Joe Davidson, *The Art of the Cigar Label* (Secaucus, N.J.: Wellfleet, 1989), 14.
4. Scarpaci, Segre, and Coyula, *Havana*, 60.

Chapter 6. A String of Public Spaces

1. Cullen, *Townscape*, 20–32.

2. Jean-Francois Lejeune, ed., *Cruelty and Utopia: Cities and Landscapes of Latin America* (New York: Princeton Architectural Press, 2005), 151–185.

3. Scarpaci, Segre, and Coyula, *Havana*, 60.

Chapter 7. Paseo del Prado

1. Lejeune, *Cruelty and Utopia*, 152.

Chapter 9. A New Urban Scale Architectural Vocabulary

1. Mumford, *City in History*, 515.

2. Ibid., 426, 515.

3. http://www.bcn.es/en/aparcatlaribal.htm.

Chapter 10. Urbanism, Culture, and Art in the Cuban Republic

1. http://www.bcn.es/en/aparcatlaribal.htm.

2. http://www.analucia.com/cities/seville/marialuisapark.htm.

3. Lejeune, *Cruelty and Utopia*, 151–185.

4. Hughes, *Barcelona*, 329.

5. Juan Bassegoda Nonell, *Antonio Gaudí: Master Architect* (New York: Abbeville Press, 2000), 10.

Chapter 11. Landmarks of Havana

1. Cathy Leff, publisher and executive editor, *Journal of Decorative and Propaganda Arts, Cuba*, theme issue no. 22 (1996): 40.

2. Pedro Martínez Inclán, *La Habana Actual: Estudios de la Capital de Cuba, desde el punto de vista de la Arquitectura de Ciudades* (Havana: P. Fernández y Cia, 1995), 265.

3. Felipe J. Préstamo Y. Hernandez, ed., *Cuba: Arquitectura Y Urbanismo*. Intro. Antonio Marcos Ramos (Miami: Ediciones Universal, 1995), 407–416.

4. Scarpaci, Segre, and Coyula, *Havana*, 299.

5. http://www.bacardi.com.

Chapter 12. The Cuban Zest for Life

1. Tropicana brochure, Alvarez y Saurina, Ave. de Truffin y Linea, Marianao, Havana.

2. Rebeca Mauleon, "Living the Legend, Mambo King Cachao Still Sparks," New York JVC Jazz Festival, 2006.

3. Edmund N. Bacon, "Archetype, Architecture," Wolfson Fellowship Lecture, College of Architecture, Art and Planning, University of Cincinnati, 1990.

Chapter 13. Characteristics of the City

Andrew Moore, (photographs), Andy Grundberg (preface), and Eduardo Luis Rodriguez (introduction), *Inside Havana* (San Francisco: Chronicle Books, 2002), 5.

2. Cullen, *Townscape*, 14.

3. Edmund N. Bacon, *Design of Cities* (New York: Viking Press, 1967), 34.

Chapter 14. Defining a Common Purpose

1. Theodore Dalrymple, *Our Culture, What's Left of It: The Mandarins and the Masses* (Chicago: Ivan R. Dee, 2005), 185.

2. Jaime Suchlicki, *Cuba: From Columbus to Castro and Beyond*, 5th ed. rev. (Washington, D.C.: Potomac Books, 2002), 166.

3. Dalrymple, *Our Culture*, 183.

4. Jane Jacobs, *The Death and Life of Great American Cities* (New York: Vintage Books, 1961), 7.

5. Ibid., 6.

6. Tom Wolfe, *From Bauhaus to Our House* (New York: Bantam Books, 1981), 56.

Bibliography

Abbate, Francesco. *Art Nouveau: The Style of the 1890s*. New York: Octopus Books, 1972.

"Ancient Havana" (pamphlet). Compliments of Nueva Fabrica de Hielo, S.A., Manufactures of Tropical Beer, Cristal Palatino Beer, and Excelsior Dark Beer, Sindicato de Artes Graficas de La Habana, S.A.

Bacon, Edmund N. *Design of Cities*. New York: Viking Press, 1967.

Barclay, Juliet. *Havana: Portrait of a City*. London: Cassell, 1993.

Bassegoda Nonell, Juan. *Antonio Gaudí: Master Architect*. New York: Abbeville Press, 2000.

Beckles, Hilary McDonald. *A History of Barbados: From Amerindian Settlement to Nation-State*. Cambridge: Cambridge University Press, 1990.

Bens Arrate, Jose Maria. *La evolución de la ciudad de La Habana desde mediados del siglo XIX hasta las primas décadas del XX*. Havana: Arquitectura Cuba, 1960.

Codrescu, Andrei. *Walker Evans: Cuba*. Intro. Judith Keller. Los Angeles: J. Paul Getty Museum, 2001.

Connors, Michael. *Cuban Elegance*. New York: Harry N. Abrams, 2004.

Cullen, Gordon. *Townscape*. New York: Reinhold, 1961.

Dalrymple, Theodore. *Our Culture, What's Left of It: The Mandarins and the Masses*. Chicago: Ivan R. Dee, 2005.

Davidson, Joe. *The Art of the Cigar Label*. Secaucus, N.J.: Wellfleet, 1989.

De Castro y de Cardelas, Martha. *El arte en Cuba*. Miami: Ediciones Universal, 1940.

Fleming, John, Hugh Honour, and Nikolaus Pevsner. *The Penguin Dictionary of Architecture*. 3rd ed. New York: Penguin Books, 1966.

Grube, Ernst J., et al. *Architecture of the Islamic World*, London: Thames and Hudson, 1978.

Hughes, Robert. *Barcelona*. New York: Alfred A. Knopf, 1992.

Inclán, Pedro Martínez. *La Habana Actual: Estudios de la Capital de Cuba, desde el punto de vista de la Arquitectura de Ciudades*. Havana: P. Fernández y Cia, 1995.

Jacobs, Jane. *The Death and Life of Great American Cities*. New York: Vintage Books, 1961.

La habana, arquitectura del siglo XX. Barcelona: Blume, 1998.

Lejeune, Jean-Francois, ed. *Cruelty and Utopia: Cities and Landscapes of Latin America*. New York: Princeton Architectural Press, 2005.

Llanes, Lillian. *Havana Then and Now*. San Diego, Calif.: Thunder Bay Press, 2004.

Markman, Sidney David. *Colonial Architecture of Antiqua Guatemala*. Philadelphia: American Philosophical Society, 1966.

Martin Zequeira, Maria Elena, and Eduardo Luis Rodriguez Fernanadez. *Guía de Arquitectura La Habana Colonial (1519–1898)*. 2nd ed. Havana: Agencia Espanola de Cooperacion Internacianal, Ciudad de la Habana, Junta de Andalucia, 1993.

Mitchell, George, ed. *Architecture of the Islamic World: Its History and Social Meaning*. London: Thames and Hudson, 1978.

Moore, Andrew (photographs), Andy Grundberg (preface), and Eduardo Luis Rodriguez (introduction). *Inside Havana*. San Francisco: Chronicle Books, 2002.

Mumford, Lewis. *The City in History: Its Origins, Its Transformations, and Its Prospects*. New York: Harcourt, Brace and World, 1961.

Préstamo Y. Hernandez, Felipe J., ed.. *Cuba: Arquitectura y Urbanismo*. Intro. Antonio Marcos Ramos. Miami: Ediciones Universal, 1995.

Ratti, Fabio. *DK Eyewitness Travel Guide Cuba*. London: DK Publishing, 2002.

Rodriguez, Eduardo Luis. *The Havana Guide: Modern Architecture, 1925–1965*. New York: Princeton Architectural Press, 2000.

Sale, Kirkpatrick. *The Conquest of Paradise: Christopher Columbus and the Columbian Legacy*. New York: Random House, 1990.

Salvads, Maria Rosa. *A Visit to the Laribal Gardens*. www.ben.es/en/aparcatlaribal.htm.

Scarpaci, Joseph L., Roberto Segre, and Mario Coyula. *Havana: Two Faces of the Antillean Metropolis*. Chapel Hill: University of North Carolina Press, 2002.

Stout, Nancy, and Jorge Rigau. *Havana, La Habana*. New York: Rizzoli, 1994.

Suchlicki, Jaime. *Cuba: From Columbus to Castro and Beyond*. 5th ed. rev. Washington, D.C.: Potomac Books, 2002.

Treister, Kenneth. *Habaneros, Photographs of the People of Havana*. Miami: Fotografas de los Habaneros, Ediciones Universal, 1997.

Weiss, Joaquin, *La arquitectura colonial cubana. Siglos XVI al XIX*. Havana: Instituto Cubano del Libro, and Seville: Juanta de Andalucía, 1996.

Wolfe, Tom. *From Bauhaus to Our House*. New York: Bantam Books, 1981.

Wright, Irene A. *Historia documental de San Cristobal de La Habana en el siglo XVI*. 2 vols. Havana: Academia de la Historia de Cuba, 1927.

Acknowledgments

The authors wish to express their deep appreciation to the following people and institutions:

Congresswoman Ileana Ros-Lehtinen; Jaime Suchlicki; John Byram; Martha Kohen; Juan Bassegoda Nonell; Eduardo Luis Rodriguez Fernandez; Juan M. Clark; Ves Spindler; John Nemmers; Kelly Byram; Carlos Alberto Montaner; Gilberto Martinez; Yleen Poblet; Catalina Préstamo; Helyne Treister; the University of Miami: Institute for Cuban and Cuban American Studies and the Otto G. Richter Library, Cuban Heritage Collection, Isabel Ezquerra; the University of Florida: Smathers Library, Archives and Manuscripts, Carl Van Ness; Digital Library Center: Lourdes Santamaria-Wheeler, Erich Kesse, Stephanie Haas, Mark Sullivan, Randall Renner; Special Collections Department: Urmi Dave, Katherine Walters, Ankit Hirdesh, Sarah Tilson, Katie Kashmiry; School of Architecture: Mary Kramer.

Index

Kenneth Treister, Fellow American Institute of Architects (FAIA), is an award-winning international architect, photographer, author, and sculptor whose work has been featured in leading art and architecture journals worldwide. He was honored with a Fellowship by the National American Institute of Architects at the Jefferson Memorial in Washington, D.C., in 1990.

Felipe J. Préstamo, the author of many scholarly publications surveying Latin American architecture including *Architecture and Urbanism in Cuba* (1995), was professor of architecture emeritus at the University of Miami, where he taught for nearly thirty years.

Raul B. Garcia is adjunct professor of architecture at Broward College, Fort Lauderdale. He has taught architecture and planning at Florida International University, Florida Atlantic University, and the University of Florida.

VIEW OF THE MALECON AND OLD FORTS AT THE ENTRANCE OF HAVANA HARBOR, CUBA

Glorieta de la Punta (bandstand at the point of the Canal de Entrada) and the Fuerte de la Punta, with the Castillo del Morro beyond, ca. 1900.